English Structure and Usage:
Book 1, Structure

Peter R. Beaven
with Erica Segal

English Structure and Usage: Book 1, Structure
Peter R. Beaven

Senior Editors:
    Katherine Webster, Erica Segal
Editor:
    Shane R. Bouchard
Contributors:
    Peter R. Beaven, Annie I. Rao, Elizabeth M. Rao, John M. Willard.
    S. James Boumil, III, Daniel A. LeClerc

Revised February 2013

The first thank you for help in putting together English Structure goes to S. James Boumil, who systematically laid out the basic principles of English grammar. Erica Segal then organized, supplemented, and enhanced his work, adding more exercises, including those that instruct in how to diagram sentences. Katharine Webster, the editor, gave the book its final review. I am indebted to all three.

Published by
The Cheshire Press
A Division of The Cheshire Group, Inc
PO Box 2090
Andover, MA 01810-0037
www.cheshirepress.com

All rights reserved. No part of this book may be
reproduced or transmitted in any form or by any means
without the express written consent of the author, except for
the inclusion of quotations in reviews.

Copyright © 2005-2014 by Beaven & Associates

ISBN: 978-0-9960210-4-3

Library of Congress Control Number: 2014956153

Printed in the United States of America

Beaven & Associates
3 Dundee Park, #202
Andover, MA 01810
978 475-5487
www.beavenandassociates.com

Beaven, Peter R.
English Structure and Usage: Book 1, Structure

Preface

English grammar, syntax, and composition are not easy to master, even for native speakers. Imagine, then, the challenges that confront today's Language Arts teachers in over-crowded public school classrooms filled with a mix of native and non-native speakers. During more than three decades of tutoring middle and high school students seeking admission to elite secondary schools and colleges, we have found that even private school pupils struggle with the finer points of grammar, syntax, and composition.

Popular culture and the computer revolution are not helping. Children today spend far less time reading books than watching television, playing electronic games, and texting. Contemporary books, which must compete with electronic media for children's attention, are more likely to be filled with conversational slang than with the complex sentences and rich vocabulary of earlier children's classics. The same advances that have led to an information explosion have resulted in an implosion of grammatical knowledge.

Hence these books on English, which teach the rules of grammar, syntax, and writing in a clear and systematic way. They also serve as workbooks, with plenty of exercises to help students identify and remedy their weak points. In the short term, these books will help middle and high school students perform better on standardized admissions tests, such as the SSAT and SAT. More importantly, they provide a strong foundation that will improve students' communication skills throughout their lives.

Book I, "Structure," covers the different parts of speech and their roles in sentences. Students will learn how to diagram sentences, which will help them avoid common errors such as: writing sentence fragments; confusing the use of "I" and "me"; and using adjectives when adverbs are appropriate. Not all students will need this volume: Those who have read well and widely, or who already have a good grasp of grammar, may prefer to go directly to Volume II, "Usage."

The lessons and exercises in these books were developed over several decades by Peter Beaven and other tutors at Beaven & Associates of Andover, Massachusetts, to help their students. We have striven to provide a clear course of study for those seeking a rigorous curriculum. We hope that teachers and students find these books useful, whether in a home-school setting or a traditional classroom, and whether they are native speakers or studying English as a second language. We also hope that the occasional quotations and excerpts from classical and contemporary literature will inspire students to read more great books – and perhaps write some enduring literature themselves.

TABLE OF CONTENTS

Chapter 1: NOUNS AND ACTION VERBS..6
   The Noun..6
   The Action Verb..10
   Putting Nouns and Verbs Together: Subjects, Direct Objects, and Indirect Objects.......12
   Diagramming..18
   Diagramming Exercises:..19

Chapter 2: ADJECTIVES, ADVERBS, AND STATE OF BEING VERBS......................22
   The Adjective..22
   The Adverb...24
   The Adverbial Objective..26
   State of Being/Linking Verbs...27
   Connecting Nouns, Adjectives, and Linking Verbs..29
   Subject and Object Complements..30
   Diagramming..31
   Diagramming Exercises..34

Chapter 3: PREPOSITIONS..36
   Diagramming..42
   Diagramming Exercises..43

Chapter 4: THE PRONOUN- BASICS...46
   Diagramming..54
   Diagramming Exercises..54

CHAPTER 5: MORE ABOUT VERBS...57
   Diagramming..68

Chapter 6: CONJUNCTIONS, INTERJECTIONS, AND DIRECT ADDRESS..............69
   Conjunctions..69
   Interjections..71
   Nouns of Direct Address...72
   Diagramming..72
   Diagramming Exercises:...74

CHAPTER 7: VERBALS AND PHRASES..77
   Phrases...77
   Appositive Phrases...77
   Verbals and Their Phrases..78
   Participial Phrases..79
   Gerund Phrases..81
   Diagramming..86
   Diagramming Exercises..87

Chapter 8: INFINITIVES..92
    Diagramming..95
    Diagramming Exercises..95

CHAPTER 9: CLAUSES..99
    Adverb Clauses..100
    Adjective Clauses..101
    Noun Clauses..103
    Indirect Questions...104
    Review: Clauses..105
    Diagramming..106
    Diagramming Exercises..109

GLOSSARY OF GRAMMATICAL TERMS..113

ANSWER KEY..116

Chapter 1: NOUNS AND ACTION VERBS

The Noun

A *noun* is a word used to name a person, place, thing, or idea. Nouns can be classified into the following subcategories:

concrete or abstract
proper or common
singular or plural
collective or not collective

A *concrete* noun refers to anything that can be discerned by one or more of the five senses, or is capable of physical measurement.

Examples: tangible things, such as *door* and *computer*;
visible things, such as *light*;
audible things, such as *sound* and *music*.
physically measureable forces, such as *electricity*.

An *abstract* noun refers to an idea, belief, quality, or characteristic. These nouns cannot be experienced directly through the senses.

Examples: feelings, such as *love*, *hatred*, *exasperation*, and *fatigue*;
ideas, such as *courage*, *capitalism*, and *perseverance*;
beliefs, such as *Catholicism* and *Hinduism*.

Note that some nouns may be *concrete* or *abstract*, depending on the definition.

Examples: *commodity*, as in "He deals in oil, coal, and other commodities,"
or "His political experience is a valuable commodity."
Commodities refers to concrete materials in the first example,
but an abstract job qualification in the second.

A *proper* noun is one that refers to a named, specific person, place, thing, or idea. Proper nouns should always be capitalized.

Examples: *Niagara Falls*, *George Lucas*, and *"Les Miserables."*

A *common* noun refers to any non-specific or general person, place, thing, or idea.

Examples: *goat*, *audacity*, *father*, *treehouse*, and *nonviolent*.

A *singular* noun refers to only one noun or entity. A singular noun need not refer to a specific noun, but it must reference only one.

Examples: *monitor*, *piece*, *clock*, and *ox*.

A *plural* noun references two or more of the same noun.

Examples: *monitors*, *pieces*, *clocks*, and *oxen*.

A *collective* noun names a group, usually treated as a single entity and taking a singular verb.

Examples: *band*, *team*, *herd*, and *committee*.

Note: Nouns can fall into multiple categories. The word herd *is a collective, singular, common, concrete noun. The word* twins *is plural, common, and concrete. The word* Buddhism *is singular, proper, and abstract.*

Exercise 1

Identify: Concrete, Abstract, or both?

1. tuna
2. conversation
3. energy
4. Ronald Reagan
5. pottery
6. loyalty
7. penguin
8. value
9. African Swallow
10. Oprah Winfrey

Exercise 2:

Identify: Common or Proper?

1. steak
2. Jesse Jackson
3. awning
4. facade
5. Anarchism

6. intelligence

7. New York City

8. The Great Gatsby

9. nation

10. Cubism

Exercise 3:

Identify: Singular or Plural?

1. diamond

2. neighborhood

3. mice

4. rage

5. group

6. leaves

7. interviews

8. water

9. molecule

10. aficionados

Exercise 4:

Identify: Collective or Not Collective?

1. jury

2. ants

3. flock

4. bunch

5. grains

6. beach

Exercise 5:

Find and underline each of the 25 nouns in this passage, excerpted from Chapter 1 of H.G. Wells's The Time Machine.

"It is simply this. That space, as our mathematicians have it, is spoken of as having three dimensions, which one may call Length, Breadth, and Thickness, and is always definable by reference to three planes, each at right angles to the others. But some philosophical people have been asking why three dimensions particularly—why not another direction at right angles to the other three – and have even tried to construct a Four-Dimension geometry. Professor Simon Newcomb was expounding this to the New York Mathematical Society only a month or so ago. You know how on a flat surface, which has only two dimensions, we can represent a figure of a three-dimensional solid, and similarly they think that by models of three dimensions they could represent one of four—if they could master the perspective of the thing. See?"

Exercise 6:

Identify and underline each of the 37 nouns in this passage excerpted from Charles Dickens's The Pickwick Papers.

"We write these words now, many miles distant from the spot at which, year after year, we met on that day, a merry and joyous circle. Many of the hearts that throbbed so gaily then, have ceased to beat; many of the looks that shone so brightly then, have ceased to glow; the hands we grasped, have grown cold; the eyes we sought, have hid their lustre in the grave; and yet the old house, the room, the merry voices and smiling faces, the jest, the laugh, the most minute and trivial circumstances connected with those happy meetings, crowd upon our mind at each recurrence of the season, as if the last assemblage had been but yesterday! Happy, happy Christmas, that can win us back to the delusions of our childish days; that can recall to the old man the pleasures of his youth; that can transport the sailor and the traveler, thousands of miles away, back to his own fireside and his quiet home!"

Exercise 7:

Categorize each noun as concrete or abstract, common or proper, singular or plural, and collective or not collective.

Example: *flower* is concrete, common, singular, and not collective

1. herd
2. Cheerios
3. boredom

4. Judaism

5. dessert

The Action Verb

A *verb* describes what is happening in a sentence. It tells you about the actions of the noun that is the subject of the sentence.

Action verbs are the type of verb that describes what a certain noun/subject does or thinks.

Examples:
>Samantha *eats* cake.
>The bird *is flying*.
>The boy *said*, "Hello!"
>The balloon *will pop*.

Notice that each of these sentences employs a verb of a different *tense*, indicating the time at which the action was, is, or will be completed. We will delve further into the topic of tense in a later chapter. For now, we will talk about a few basic tenses.

The *present tense* is used to denote an action that is occurring right now, or to make a general statement about something.

Examples:
>The sun *shines* often in the desert.
>→ The present tense verb *shines* allows us to make a general statement about the desert sun.
>
>Mr. Smith *grades* his students on a pass/fail basis.
>→ The verb *grades* is in the present, but Mr. Smith isn't necessarily grading papers or tests as we speak; this is a general statement.
>
>J.K. Rowling *writes* books about teenage wizards.
>→ This sentence is similar to the previous example; J.K. Rowling may not be writing at this very moment, but this is a general statement about the kind of books she writes.

The *present progressive* tense is used to describe ongoing action – something which continues to be carried out as the speaker speaks – or to describe an action that will happen in the near future.

Examples:
>The farmer *is planting* his seeds.
>→ The present progressive verb *is planting* indicates that this is an ongoing activity, even if it's not happening at this exact minute because the farmer has paused to eat lunch.
>
>Jenna *is telling* jokes.

→ The present progressive verb *is telling* indicates an action that is happening now.

The plane *is landing* in half an hour.
→ The present progressive verb *is landing* indicates an action that will occur in the near future.

Sometimes an instantaneous action can be communicated by using either the present *or* the present progressive.

Example:
Look how fast the dancer *spins*.
Look how fast the dancer *is spinning*.
→ Both sentences convey a sense of an immediate present.

Exercise 8:

Underline all the verbs in the following sentences and identify them as present, present progressive, or neither.

1. Sarah cooks a lot of pizza in her free time.
2. It rained cats and dogs last night.
3. That pig is giving birth to piglets!
4. My mother uses the treadmill every morning.
5. When Julia drinks water instead of soda, she loses weight.
6. Because Melissa worked very hard in high school, she attends an excellent college.
7. That boy made a lot of money when he mowed his neighbor's lawn last summer.
8. Mr. Jones really wants a raise, so he is working extra hours at the office.
9. Liz was studying physics when the phone rang.
10. Colleges look for students who participate in a wide range of activities.

Exercise 9:

Write two completely different sentences with each verb, one in the present and one in the present progressive.

Example: send

The girl *sends* letters to her parents every week. (present)

John *is sending* the model train to the winning bidder on eBay. (present progressive)

1. read
2. surround

3. annoy

4. buy

5. build

Exercise 10:

Circle the correct form of the verb.

1. My sister eats/is eating lunch every day at noon.

2. John first washes his face; then he brushes/is brushing his teeth.

3. Rose thinks someone knocks/is knocking at the door.

4. My teacher sometimes takes/is taking points away for misspelled words.

5. Every morning, Amanda watches/is watching the news.

6. Look over there! The show starts/is starting!

7. Quiet! Students take/are taking an exam in the next room!

8. Michelle often eats/is eating pancakes for breakfast.

9. The girl surfs/is surfing the Internet.

Putting Nouns and Verbs Together: Subjects, Direct Objects, and Indirect Objects

Nouns and verbs serve as the most basic elements of a sentence. All sentences must contain a subject, the "who" or "what" that does the action of the verb. The subject is a noun or pronoun (I, they, she, it, or we are examples of pronouns, which will be discussed in more detail later).

Examples:
>*Susan* is giving a gift.
>*Flowers* bloom in the springtime.
>*Muslims* pray to Allah.

Notice that all the subjects are the *doers* of the action verb that follows.

Exercise 11:

Use each noun as the subject of a sentence. Use action verbs.

1. cheese

2. Jack

3. dictionaries

4. dogs

5. Christians

Exercise 12:

Underline the subject of each sentence.

1. The paperboy delivers the New York Times.

2. Are the cookies burning?

3. Sasha eats a lot of pasta.

4. The train is departing.

Let's look back at an earlier example sentence: *Susan is giving a gift*. We established that *Susan* is the subject, because she performs the action of the verb: She is the giver. To put it another way, if we were to ask, "Who is giving the gift?" the answer would be *Susan;* she is the "who" of the sentence. But *Susan* is not the only noun in the sentence. What about *gift*? The word *gift* is the object of the verb, and more specifically, a direct object (DO). Direct objects are people and things that receive the action of a verb, telling us who or what is affected by the verb. Below are some examples of sentences with direct objects (in italics).

Examples:
People wear *clothing*. (People do the wearing; clothing is the thing *being worn*)
Josh completes his *homework* every night. (Josh is the person who completes; homework is the thing *being completed*)
My dad is boiling *water* for tea. (My dad is doing the boiling; water is the thing *being boiled*)
Sally hates *Alicia*. (Sally does the hating; Alicia is the person *being hated*)

Exercise 13:

Underline the subject and circle the direct object in each sentence.

1. The chef is preparing a salad.

2. The diner leaves a tip.

3. The author is writing a novel.

4. College students drink a lot of coffee.

5. The boy dropped the basketball.

6. Sean plays basketball very well.

7. My teacher tells a lot of stories in class.

8. The Gap sells good-quality jeans to people of all ages.

9. The man ate the cow.

10. The shark ate the man.

Exercise 14:

Write a sentence for each set of nouns, using the first noun as the subject and the second noun as a direct object.

Example: Girls, dresses → Girls wear dresses to fancy parties.

1. Jared, baseball

2. clown, balloon

3. baby, mug

4. Ellen, music

5. Mary, curtains

6. customer, bag

7. man, lion

8. lion, man

Returning to "Susan is giving a gift," we might logically ask, "To whom is she giving that gift?" Let's suppose she's giving it to someone named Jerry. The sentence becomes: "Susan is giving Jerry a gift." Jerry is the sentence's *indirect object*—it answers the question "to or for whom?" or "to or for what?"

Some examples of sentences with direct and indirect objects (DO is in italics, IO is in bold):

Examples:
    Melissa showed her **mother** her *bruise*. (What's being shown? The bruise. To whom? To her mother.)
    Jacob offers **Jesse** a *bagel*. (What's being offered? A bagel. To whom? To Jesse.)
    My mother is giving the floor a good scrubbing. (What's mother giving? A scrubbing. To what? To the floor.)
    The Jacksons give their **children** *money*. (What's being given? Money. To whom? To children.)

*If it helps, you can often reword a sentence to help you distinguish between the DO and the IO. For instance, if you are confused by a sentence like the second example above, you can think of it as "Jacob offers a bagel to Jesse." The fact that Jesse is the IO becomes clearer when the word "to" is actually in the sentence. When you are confused, it also helps to return to basic questions. For a DO, ask yourself, "What is actually receiving the action of the verb?" In this example, Jesse is NOT receiving the action;

Jesse himself is not being offered—the bagel is.

Certain verbs act as clues that there may be an indirect object coming up. Verbs having to do with giving, telling, offering, and showing can and often do take indirect objects.

Examples:
    The father gave **Derek** a *spanking*. (Gave what? A spanking. To whom? To Derek.)
    Hannah is offering her **sister** *help*. (Offering what? Help. To whom? To her sister.)
    The Constitution grants **Americans** *rights*. ("Grants" has a sense of giving. Grants what? Rights. To whom? To Americans.)
    Waiters serve restaurant **guests** *lunch*. ("Serve" has a sense of giving and offering. Serve what? Lunch. To whom? To guests.)

Notice also that certain sentences don't *require* indirect objects, and they still make logical sense without the IO.

Examples:
    The father gave a spanking.
    Hannah is offering help.
    The Constitution grants rights.
    Waiters serve lunch.

The indirect object simply provides additional information.

In a later chapter, we will examine the distinction between an indirect object and the object of a preposition. However, it is worth noting that when you reword sentences as above, you turn the indirect object into the object of the preposition "to."

Example:
    Judy gave Tom flowers. → Tom is the indirect object.
    Judy gave flowers to Tom. → Tom is the object of the preposition "to."

Exercise 15:

In each sentence, underline the direct object, if there is one, and circle the indirect object, if there is one.

1. Peter gives his wife a bouquet.

2. Jean is bringing Michael his dinner.

3. The gymnast wins a trophy.

4. Jamie is drinking soda.

5. Tom hugs Judy.

6. Tom gives a hug to Judy.

7. The cat is chasing the squirrel.

8. Joe pays money to the cashier.

9. Joe pays the cashier.

10. Isabelle tells her mother lies.

11. Ms. Foster shows her student the answer.

12. The boy is going to the mall.

13. The grocer gives the receipt to the customer.

14. Jake offers his girlfriend a ride home.

15. Peter reads Eugene a book.

16. Peter reads to Eugene.

17. The secretary brings my clients coffee.

Exercise 16:

Write a sentence using the first noun as a direct object and the second noun, if there is one, as an indirect object.

1. book, Josh
2. flowers
3. sweater, Ian
4. New York
5. eraser, John
6. car, family
7. race car
8. curtains
9. salary, Rachel
10. dinner, queen
11. William
12. water, runner

Exercise 17:

Use each noun in two sentences. In the first, use it as a direct object. In the second, use it as an indirect object. Try to vary your sentences!

Example: tutor
>Sam greets the tutor. (tutor is the DO)
>Sam shows his tutor the completed assignment. (tutor is the IO)

1. Lila

2. man

3. doctor

4. student

5. Penelope

6. child

7. teacher

8. mother

Action verbs take two forms: transitive and intransitive. When an action verb takes an object, it is called a *transitive* verb, from the Latin word *transire,* which means *to go over* or *across.* The verb is carrying the action toward something or someone: the object.

Examples:
>The principal punished the rebellious students.
>Apples give Johnny a stomachache.
>The women found the museum.
>The outfielder caught the ball.
>Lauren bought a mini-skirt.
>Cara washes her car.
>The twins broke the computer.

Notice that the above sentences would not be complete without an object. Notice that transitive verbs do not make sense without objects:

Examples:
>The principal punished.
>Apples give.
>The women found.
>The outfielder caught.
>Lauren bought.
>Cara washes.
>The twins broke.

When an action verb does not take an object, it is called an *intransitive* verb.

Examples:
    The newborn baby cried.
    In October my SAT scores increased.
    The professor sneezed loudly.
    Last night the old man died.
    I went to the store. (You might think that store is the direct object, but it is the object of the preposition *to*, not the object of the verb.)

Some verbs can be both transitive *and* intransitive, depending on their use.

Examples:

He ate greedily.	Intransitive
He ate steak.	Transitive (Ate what? Steak.)
He runs every morning.	Intransitive
He runs marathons.	Transitive (Runs what? Marathons.)
He is leaving soon.	Intransitive
He is leaving the house.	Transitive (Leaving what? The house.)
He moves quickly.	Intransitive
He moves boxes around.	Transitive (Moves what? Boxes.)

Exercise 18:

In the following sentences, identify each verb as transitive or intransitive. If the verb is transitive, underline the direct object.

1. Johnathan is kicking the ball.

2. The monster is eating Shane for breakfast.

3. The monster ate quickly.

4. Now, he has a stomachache.

5. The boy bought books from the store.

6. The toddler wailed all night long.

7. Van Gogh paints in his studio.

8. Yolanda really loves Monopoly.

Diagramming

Sentences can be analyzed and broken down into their various grammatical elements by creating sentence diagrams. As we discuss each new part of the sentence, we will also explain the proper method for diagramming it.

Here are a few basic guidelines for diagramming sentences. In any diagram, the *simple subject* (excluding all modifiers, which we'll discuss in the next chapter) is placed on a horizontal sentence line to the left of a vertical line that crosses it. The verb is placed to the right of the vertical line.

Example: Jack ran.

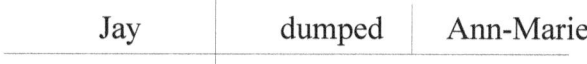

The noun *Jack* is the subject of the sentence. The verb is *ran*. The vertical line that passes through the horizontal sentence line separates the subject from the verb.

Direct objects sit on the sentence line to the right of the verb, separated from the verb with a vertical line that touches, but does not cross, the sentence line.

Example: Jay dumped Ann-Marie.

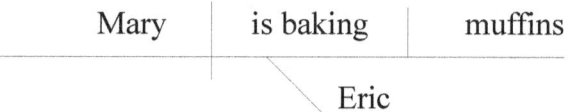

Jay is the subject of the sentence; *dumped* is the verb. *Ann-Marie* is the direct object of the transitive verb *dumped (Who was dumped? Ann-Marie)*.

Indirect objects are diagrammed by connecting a horizontal line to the verb with a diagonal line, beneath the sentence line.

Example: Mary is baking Eric muffins.

```
     Mary  |  is baking  |  muffins
                \ Eric
```

Mary is the subject of the sentence; *is baking* is the transitive verb (in the present progressive tense). *Muffins* is the direct object of the verb *baking*. *Eric*, the indirect object, is placed on a horizontal line, below and diagonally connected to the verb.

Note that questions are diagrammed the same way as statements. Regardless of where the subject and verb fall in the question, they are diagrammed with the subject to the left, the verb to the right. This can be a little tricky at first, especially as the verb may be split in certain tenses, but the principal holds: subject to the left, verb to the right.

Example: Does Mary like Peter?

Mary	Does like	Peter

Does like is the verb (the tense is the present emphatic), and *Does* is capitalized because it's the first word in the sentence.

Diagramming Exercises:

Now it's your turn! Try diagramming the following sentences yourself.

1. Flowers bloom.

2. People breathe air.

3. Do dogs swim?

4. Girls are eating pie.

5. Jane gives Sarah gifts.

6. Ben is running.

7. Ben is running races.

8. Veronica dribbles basketballs.

9. Whales eat plankton.

10. Children give Mrs. Benson headaches.

11. Amanda bakes children cookies.

12. Doreen is buying Jake dinner.

Chapter 2: ADJECTIVES, ADVERBS, AND STATE OF BEING VERBS

The Adjective

An *adjective* is any word that modifies or describes a noun, pronoun (you'll learn about these in a later chapter), or another adjective. An adjective can answer any of the following questions:

What kind?   *white* desk, *large* elephant, *old* man, *fuzzy* slippers, *hot* coffee, *smart* student

Example: *Short* girls make *good* gymnasts.
→ What kind of girls? *Short* ones. What kind of gymnasts do they make? *Good* ones.

Which one?   *this* chair, *that* ball, *a* balloon, *the* giraffe

Example: *This* boy likes *that* girl.
→ Which boy? *This* boy. Which girl does he like? *That* girl.

How many or how much?   *four* boys, *many* occurrences, *twenty* students, *several* homes

Example: *Three* boys can make *many* messes!
→ How many boys? *Three*. How many messes can they make? *Many*.

Articles are the most common form of adjective. The articles are: *a*, *an*, and *the*. They tell you whether the noun or pronoun that they modify refers to something definite (the) or indefinite (a, an). A definite article precedes a noun referring to a particular person, place, thing, or idea, while an indefinite article precedes a noun referring to any member of a group.

Examples: Give Harry *a* book.
→ The use of the indefinite article shows that we are referring to *any* book; we don't have a specific one in mind.

Give Harry *the* book.
→ The use of the definite article shows that we have a specific book in mind.

Jen wants *a* pony.
→ The indefinite article *a* conveys the general statement that Jen would like to have a pony, any pony. We don't know which specific pony she wants.

This is *the* pony Jen wants.
→ The definite article is used here because we are referring to the *specific* pony that Jen

wants.

Whether to use *a* or *an* depends on the sound that begins the next word.
  - When the singular noun begins with a consonant, use *a*

    Examples: a boy, a girl, a pony, a fish, a bowl, a building, a computer

  - When the singular noun begins with a vowel, use *an*

    Examples: an apple, an eggplant, an octopus, an igloo, an umbrella

  - When the singular noun begins with a consonant *sound*, use *a*

    Examples: a European, a university, a user

Demonstrative adjectives allow us to reference a particular and specific item. *This* and *that* are the singular demonstrative adjectives, and *these* and *those* are the plural forms.

Examples:
  Dylan wants *this* sweater. (not just any old sweater...*this* sweater)
  Those children are screaming. (again, not just any children...*those* children)

Exercise 1:

In the following passage from Emily Bronte's Wuthering Heights, *underline all 12 adjectives. (You do not have to underline articles or possessives.)*

"The moon shone bright; a sprinkling of snow covered the ground, and I reflected that she might, possibly, have taken it into her head to walk about the garden, for refreshment. I did detect a figure creeping along the inner fence of the park; but it was not my young mistress: on its emerging into the light, I recognized one of the grooms. He stood a considerable period, viewing the carriage-road through the grounds; then started off at a brisk pace, as if he had detected something, and reappeared presently, leading Miss's pony; and there she was, just dismounted, and walking by its side. The man took his charge stealthily across the grass towards the stable. Cathy entered by the casement window of the drawing room, and glided noiselessly up to where I awaited her. She put the door gently to, slipped off her snowy shoes, untied her hat, and was proceeding, unconscious of my espionage, to lay aside her mantle, when I suddenly rose and revealed myself. The surprise petrified her an instant: she uttered an inarticulate exclamation, and stood fixed."

Exercise 2:

Write sentences using the following words as adjectives.

1. dark
2. rare
3. bright
4. hot
5. dizzying
6. joyful
7. breathtaking
8. youthful
9. enormous
10. smelly

The Adverb

An *adverb* may modify a verb, adjective, or other adverb. It is commonly used to describe how, where, when, or to what extent the action of a verb is carried out. Many adverbs end in *-ly*, but not all. Perhaps the most commonly used adverb is *not*.

Examples:

Sandra left the house *quickly* after the fire alarm sounded. (*How* did Sandra leave? *Quickly*. The adverb *quickly* describes the manner in which the verb is carried out.)

The chef is buying fresh vegetables *today*. (*When* is the chef buying fresh vegetables? *Today*. The adverb *today* describes when the verb is taking place. Note that *today* can also be a noun or an adjective.)

My cat does not like wet food. (*How* does the cat like wet food? *Not*. The adverb *not* modifies the verb *like* by negating it.)

Frank *often* studies in the library. (*How frequently* does Frank study in the library? *Often*. The adverb *often* describes how frequently the verb is carried out.)

Jillian went to church *there* when she was younger. (*Where* did Jillian go to church? *There*. The adverb *there* describes where the verb took place. Note that *there* can also be a pronoun or an adjective.)

Adverbs may also be used to describe adjectives.

Examples:
>When standing on a boat's prow, one must be *extremely* careful not to fall overboard. (How careful? *Extremely* careful. The adverb *extremely* describes the adjective *careful*.)
>
>Yo Yo Ma is an *exceptionally* talented cellist. (*How* talented? *Exceptionally* talented.)
>
>Adrian wears *very* expensive clothes. (*How* expensive? *Very* expensive.)

Adverbs can also modify other adverbs.

Examples:
>Laura danced *very* gracefully. (The original adverb *gracefully* tells us how Laura danced. The second adverb *very* tells us *how* gracefully she danced.)
>
>Turtles move *quite* slowly. (The original adverb *slowly* tells us how turtles move. The second adverb *quite* tells us *how* slowly they move.)
>
>It's *not* likely that she will get the job. (The original adverb *likely* tells us how probable it is that she will get the job. The second adverb *not* tells us the probability is low.)

Notice that many adverbs, such as *gracefully* and *slowly*, look like adjectives plus an "*-ly*" ending. Adverbs frequently end in "*-ly*," but many do not, and many words that do end in "*-ly*" are not adverbs.
>Examples of adverbs that *do not* end in "-ly": very, often, well, quite, high, seldom
>Examples of words that *do* end in "-ly" and are not adverbs: friendly, fatherly, lonely, lovely

Exercise 3:

Underline the adverbs in the following sentences and note what part of speech they modify.

1. Adam walked stealthily across the capture-the-flag field.
2. Hilary waved very shyly at Josh.
3. Josephina, who was very upset with Nathan, kicked him.
4. Thomas made his parents dinner yesterday.
5. Brian loves Rita intensely.
6. Peter is an exceedingly attractive man.
7. Bridget is not studying math.
8. Abby acted quite well in her school play.
9. Amy always wears flip flops.

10. Nina was clearly baffled by his question.
11. Jill is taking the SAT tomorrow.

Exercise 4:

Write sentences using the following adverbs. Note what part of speech the adverb modifies.

1. Gently
2. Quite
3. Extremely
4. Always
5. Never
6. Well
7. Apparently
8. Here
9. Softly
10. Rarely

Adverbial Objective

Sometimes a noun or a group of words containing a noun can be used as an adverb because it answers the same question an adverb would answer: how, where, when, or to what extent.

Examples:
    When did the baby fall asleep *last night*?
    Mom is leaving for China *next week*.
        (Both of these examples answer the question: When? In these examples, the verb is modified.)

    The soldiers are coming *this way*.
        (*This way* answers the question: Where are they coming?)

    The senator worries *a lot*.
    Elizabeth likes this sweater *the best*.
        (Both of these examples answer the question: To what extent does the action of the verb take place?)

    The hike is *five miles* long.

(*Five miles* describes the adjective *long*. It answers: To what extent is it long?)

Exercise 5:

Underline adverbs and adverbial objectives. Identify whether you have underlined an adverb, an adverbial objective, or both.

1. Come here!
2. Come this way!
3. Tomorrow Lauren is going to the store.
4. Vicky is moving to New York next Wednesday.
5. Tammy deposited the paycheck the next day.
6. Jason never says hello.
7. Penny lives next door.
8. Kelly is extremely beautiful.
9. Kelly is 24 years old.
10. Sometimes Ned drives a different way.
11. Wilma and George often talk all night.
12. The pool is nearly ten feet deep.

State of Being/Linking Verbs

State of being verbs, or *linking verbs*, do not express an action taken by the subject. Instead, they serve to link the subject with a descriptive term.

Some common linking verbs are:
appear	is	seem	taste
become	look	smell	
feel	remain	sound	

Examples:
The girl *is* a student. (*Is* connects the subject, girl, to more information describing her.)
The water *seemed* cold. (*Seemed* connects the subject, water, to more information about it.)
This pizza *tastes* bad. (*Tastes* connects the subject, pizza, to more information describing it.)
This test *looks* easy. (*Looks* connects the subject, test, to additional information about it.)

State of being verbs essentially act as equal signs.

Examples:
    Joe is a plumber.   Joe = plumber
    The music is loud.   The music = loud
    The situation seems dangerous.   The situation = dangerous
    The bread turned moldy.   The bread = moldy
    Lana feels sick.   Lana = sick

When the verb *to be* stands alone, it is always a linking verb. Some verbs, however, can serve as either linking verbs *or* action verbs. These verbs include: appear, feel, grow, look, prove, remain, smell, sound, taste, and turn.

Examples:
    John smells pizza.   Action verb
    John smells bad.   Linking verb

    Rhonda tastes the milk.   Action verb
    The milk tastes sour.   Linking verb

If you can substitute a form of the verb to be (is, are, etc.) or an equal sign and the sentence still makes sense, the verb is acting as a linking verb. Let's look at the second set of examples above:

    Rhonda tastes the milk.
    → We can't rewrite this as "Rhonda is the milk" or Rhonda = milk; therefore, the verb is
        functioning as an action verb.

    The milk tastes sour.
    → When we rewrite this as "The milk is sour" or milk = sour, we still have something that
        makes sense; therefore, the verb is acting as a linking verb.

Exercise 6:

Identify verbs as action or linking.

1. Joseph is a skilled doctor.
2. Sandy dances like a rock star.
3. Pedro bakes great cookies.
4. This lake is too cold for swimming.
5. This school seems like a good fit.
6. Jacob smells bad.
7. Jacob smells a gas leak.
8. Ms. Samuels complains frequently.

9. Dan looked calm in the face of adversity.

10. Jan is growing a tail!

11. Jan's tail is long!

12. Sylvester seemed pale in the bright sunlight.

Exercise 7:

Write two sentences for each verb, using it as an action verb in the first sentence and as a linking verb in the second.

1. appear   action:

                linking:

2. look   action:

                linking:

3. grow   action:

                linking:

4. prove   action:

                linking:

5. remain   action:

                linking:

6. sound   action:

                linking:

7. turn   action:

                linking:

Connecting Nouns, Adjectives, and Linking Verbs

If a noun is separated from a subject by a linking verb, it is called a *predicate nominative* (PN).

Examples:
>Herbert is a *farmer*.
>Seeds become *trees*.

If an adjective is separated from its noun by a linking verb, it is called a *predicate adjective* (PA).

Examples:
>Herbert is *tall*.
>People grow *old*.
>This milk tastes *terrible*.
>Janet feels *exhausted*.

Exercise 8:

Write sentences using the following words as either predicate nominatives or predicate adjectives, depending on the part of speech. Note whether you have used a PN or a PA in each sentence. Try to use verbs other than to be *whenever you can.*

1. tiny
2. obnoxious
3. kangaroo
4. cheese
5. American
6. beautiful
7. foul

Subject and Object Complements

Another word for predicate nominatives and predicate adjectives is *subject complements*. Linking verbs use subject complements to complete their meanings, because they link a subject to another word that describes the subject.

Sometimes, an action verb may need more information to complete its meaning. In this case, the word that refers to the direct object is known as the *object complement*. The object complement renames or further describes the direct object.

Example:
>They appointed Arnold Schwarzenegger.
>They appointed Arnold Schwarzenegger ***governor***.

The word *governor*, the object complement, adds information: the position to which Arnold Schwarzenegger was appointed. Some sentences make no sense when stripped of the object complement.

Examples:
    Many consider New York ***a sophisticated city***.
    They named the baby ***Isabelle***.
    The movie made my parents ***sad***.

Exercise 9:

Underline subject and object complements. Write an S over subject complements and an O over object complements. Hint: Figure out whether the verb is a linking or an action verb.

1. Bob appeared very unkempt.
2. Ryan painted his old car orange.
3. The small rabbit was white.
4. Purple is my favorite color.
5. The junior class elected the foreign exchange student president.
6. Health is a major concern.
7. The fast girl was the first-place winner.
8. I consider him hardworking and talented.
9. She is a pretty girl.
10. Steven called him a liar.

Diagramming

Now that you've learned more parts of speech, or grammatical terms, you can start applying them to the diagramming rules you learned in Chapter 1.

Adjectives are placed on diagonal lines that extend below and to the right of the words they modify. *Adverbs* are placed on similar lines below their respective verbs, or next to their respective adverbs or adjectives, depending on what they modify.

Examples:
    The ice cream is melting slowly.

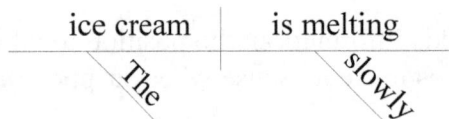

The article *The* modifies the subject *ice cream*, so we attach it to *ice cream* on a diagonal line. The adverb *slowly* modifies the verb *is melting*, so we attach it to *is melting* on a diagonal line. Notice that on the diagram, we capitalize the sentence's first word, in this case *The*.

The extremely obnoxious girl shouts.

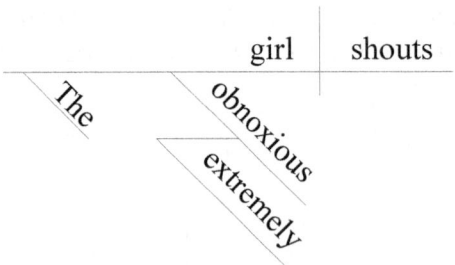

The and *obnoxious* are both adjectives modifying *girl*, so they are connected to *girl* with diagonal lines. The adverb *extremely* modifies the adjective *obnoxious*, so it is connected to *obnoxious* with a diagonal line.

Linking verbs are diagrammed the same way as action verbs; they are separated from their subjects by a vertical line that crosses through the base line.

Predicate nominatives and *predicate adjectives* are diagrammed the same way; they are separated from their linking verbs by a backslashed line that does not cross the base line.

Examples:
Patricia is a redhead.

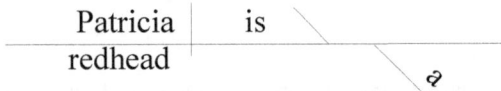

Patricia is the subject of the sentence, so we separate it from its linking verb *is*. *Redhead* is a predicate nominative, as it is a noun modifying *Patricia* separated by a linking verb. The article *a* modifies *redhead*.

These dirty children smell terrible.

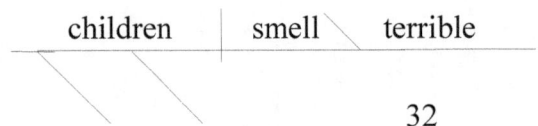

Children is the subject of the sentence, and *smell* is the verb. The adjective *terrible* enables us to see that *smell* is acting as a linking verb (children = terrible makes sense), and therefore, *terrible* is a predicate adjective. *These* and *dirty* are both adjectives modifying *children*. *These* is capitalized because it is the first word of the sentence.

These dirty children smell terribly.

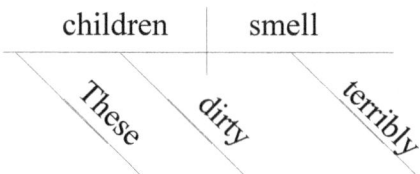

As in the sentence above, *children* is the subject of the sentence, and *smell* is the verb. The adverb *terribly* modifies the verb *smell*. *These* and *dirty* modify children. Although we need not denote whether *smell* is a linking or action verb in order to complete the diagram, it is important to try to make that distinction. Linking verbs serve to connect a noun to another word that describes them, whether that word is an adjective or another noun. But the diagram helps us see that *smell* isn't connecting *children* to anything at all; therefore, it is acting as an intransitive action verb. The adverb simply tells us *how* the children *smell—terribly*. Perhaps they have colds and their noses are stuffed up?

Adverbial objectives are diagrammed by placing the noun on a horizontal line and any modifiers on a diagonal line.

Parker is going that way.

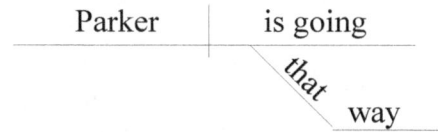

That way is an adverbial objective. *Way* is a noun, and *that* modifies it.

Object complements are placed on the sentence line before the direct object, preceded by a backslash.

The committee appointed James chairman.

```
    committee  | appointed / chairman
 James         |
```

Committee is the subject of this sentence (modified by *the*), and *appoints* is the verb. *James* is the direct object. In this sentence, however, we also have an object complement—*chairman*. *Chairman* renames and further describes *James*. Therefore, we place *chairman* in between the verb and the direct object. We use a slash between the object complement and the verb, and the normal direct object line between the object complement and the direct object.

Diagramming Exercises

Diagram the following sentences on your own.

1. Ron is a doctor.

2. Ron is a good doctor.

3. Jane is very beautiful.

4. Is Jane very beautiful?

5. The old computer is working very slowly.

6. The very old computer is working slowly.

7. These dirty children smell pizza.

8. The very loud babies are quietly eating extremely mushy peas.

9. The new puppies are often extremely energetic.

10. Daniel is quite an excellent student.

11. The young American girls are quickly eating a small supper.

12. Sam is coming this way.

13. Patricia is making Rhonda crazy!

14. The pretty girl is giving the exceedingly handsome boy a kiss.

Chapter 3: PREPOSITIONS

A preposition connects nouns and phrases (and pronouns, as we'll see later) to other words, forming *prepositional phrases*. Prepositional phrases provide us with additional information about a noun by showing location, position, duration, possession, etc.

Examples (the prepositional phrases are in brackets; the prepositions are in boldface):
    The frog leaped [**over** the hot fire].
    June sat [**beside** Jane].
    [**In** the month] [**of** June], it rarely snows [**in** Massachusetts].
    Bob will go home [**after** the show].
    [**Under** the table], Pam is reading a book [**about** purple giraffes].

Notice that the prepositional phrases are formed by adding nouns (and sometimes adjectives modifying those nouns, like "hot fire" and "purple giraffes") to the preposition. What we then get is a sense of a relationship, whether it has do with space, time, ownership, subject matter, etc.

Examples:
    the book [**on** the wood table] → gives us a sense of space, location
    a nap [**before** dinner] → gives us a sense of time
    the school [**of** the deaf] → gives us a sense of ownership, possession
    a day [**with** my friends] → gives us a sense of accompaniment and relationship
    the boy [**with** bright blue eyes] → gives us a sense of ownership and description
    approach [**with** caution] → gives us a sense of manner
    the man who looks [**like** Paul Newman] → gives us a sense of similarity

Commonly used prepositions:

about	below	for	throughout
above	beneath	from	to
across	beside	in	toward
after	besides	into	under
against	between	like	underneath
along	beyond	of	until
amid	but	off	unto
among	by	on	up
around	concerning	over	upon
at	down	past	with
before	during	since	within
behind	except	through	without

Exercise 1:

Write a prepositional phrase using each of the following prepositions. The phrases may contain adjectives, but adjectives are not required.

Example: concerning → concerning your proposal

1. above
2. after
3. around
4. at
5. behind
6. beneath
7. between
8. down
9. during
10. from
11. into
12. off
13. over
14. throughout
15. toward
16. until
17. upon
18. within

Exercise 2:

Write a prepositional phrase using each of the following prepositions and at least one article that is not an adjective.

Example: after → after a delicious dinner

1. about
2. across
3. among

4. beside

5. beyond

6. over

7. past

8. to

9. underneath

10. without

Exercise 3:

In each sentence, underline the preposition(s) and bracket the prepositional phrase or phrases.

1. Carrie is walking into the room.
2. Dylan sits on the chair.
3. The chair collapses under Dylan.
4. Carrie is laughing at Dylan.
5. Helga runs to the kitchen from the bedroom.
6. Jessie's cousin swims in the pond.
7. After the shopping trip, Lucy was broke.
8. Lizzie is walking on the path with her dog.
9. Jay's friend is going to Phillips Exeter Academy.
10. Adrian is writing in black ink.
11. Before each performance, Pam gargles with salt water.
12. The boy from New Mexico is traveling into space.
13. Mr. Johnson is a professor of mathematics at a prestigious university.
14. The CD is on the desk in the bedroom.
15. During periods of rain, Terry reads books about cooking.

Exercise 4:

In the following passage excerpted from Herman Melville's Moby Dick, *underline all 26 prepositions and bracket the prepositional phrases. Be careful to distinguish between "to" as a preposition and "to" acting as part of the infinitive form of a verb, such as "to be" or "to inquire."*

"It was quite late in the evening when the little Moss came snugly to anchor, and Queequeg and

I went ashore; so we could attend to no business that day, at least none but a supper and a bed. The landlord of the Spouter Inn had recommended us to his cousin Hosea Hussey of the Try Pots, whom he asserted to be the proprietor of one of the best kept hotels in all Nantucket, and moreover he had assured us that Cousin Hosea, as he called him, was famous for his chowders. In short, he plainly hinted that we could not possibly do better than try potluck at the Try Pots. But the directions he had given us about keeping a yellow warehouse on our starboard hand till we opened a white church to the larboard, and then keeping that on the larboard hand till we made a corner three points to the starboard, and that done, then ask the first man we met where the place was: these crooked directions of his very much puzzled us at first, especially as, at the outset, Queequeg insisted that the yellow warehouse--our first point of departure--must be left on the larboard hand, whereas I had understood Peter Coffin to say it was on the starboard. However, by dint of beating about a little in the dark, and now and then knocking up a peaceable inhabitant to inquire the way, we at last came to something which there was no mistaking."

The noun in the prepositional phrase is called the *object of the preposition*.

Examples:
>throughout the sweltering *summer*
>down the icy *slope*
>into a mysterious *forest*

Exercise 5:

Use each noun as the object of a preposition in an original sentence. Bracket the prepositional phrase. Try not to use any preposition more than once.

Example: door → I walk [through the door].

1. library

2. night

3. mother

4. roof

5. hesitation

6. crowd

7. stairs

8. exam

9. river

10. April

Just like adjectives and adverbs, prepositional phrases provide us with additional information. We must then figure out what word the prepositional phrase is modifying.

Sometimes a prepositional phrase describes a noun. We call this kind of prepositional phrase an *adjective phrase* because it serves the same role as an adjective.

Examples:
> The boy [with blue eyes] is eating spaghetti. (*With blue eyes* describes the *boy*, a noun)
> The dog [in the kennel] bit the attendant. (*In the kennel* describes the *dog*, a noun)
> The northern part [of Maine] is quite scenic. (*Of Maine* describes *part*, a noun)

Sometimes a prepositional phrase modifies a verb. We call this kind of prepositional phrase an *adverb phrase* because it serves the same role as an adverb.

Examples:
> He left his homework [on the counter]. (*On the counter* answers the question, "Where was it left?")
> Olivia is returning home [after a blind date]. (*After a blind date* describes when the verb *returning* is taking place.)
> Jared studies the textbook [with great care]. (*With great care* describes the manner in which the verb *studies* is carried out.)

Exercise 6:

Bracket each prepositional phrase. Determine whether each prepositional phrase is an adverb phrase or an adjective phrase.

1. Sally is getting married in New York City.

2. The eye of the storm is approaching.

3. Jeff is going to the movies.

4. The mother is putting gifts under the Christmas tree.

5. This is a large portion of pancakes.

6. Randy needs a key for the front door.

7. Laura is hanging out with friends.

8. The drawer with the important files is locked.

9. The girl with big ears is listening.

10. The girl is listening with her big ears.

Exercise 7:

Write a sentence using the prepositional phrase(s) as directed. If there are two, they can be used in any order.

1. under the wallpaper *as an adjective*

2. above her bed *as an adverb*

3. into the box *as an adverb*

4. with intricate stitching *as an adjective*

5. around the house *as an adjective*, in a garbage bag *as an adverb*

6. within the lines *as an adverb*

7. among his peers *as an adverb*, for his intelligence *as an adverb*

8. between the chairs *as an adjective*, around the room *as an adjective*

9. despite her bad temper *as an adverb*

10. beyond the horizon *as an adjective*

Exercise 8:

For each prepositional phrase, write two sentences, one using the phrase as an adjective and one using the phrase as an adverb. Denote which is which.

1. along the shore

2. across the river

3. between the girls

4. on the spaghetti

5. through the keyhole

Diagramming

Now that you have learned what prepositional phrases are and how they function, you are ready to add them to your diagramming repertoire! Prepositions are diagrammed just like adjectives and adverbs; the preposition is placed on a diagonal line connected to the word the prepositional phrase modifies. This is why you must be able to distinguish between an adjective phrase and an adverb phrase! The object of the preposition is then placed on a horizontal line connected to the preposition's diagonal line. The whole phrase looks a bit like an arm coming off of the modified word. Any article or adjective that modifies the object of the preposition is then diagrammed exactly the way you learned how to diagram articles and adjectives in the previous chapter.

Examples:

Aaron leaves the keys on the counter.

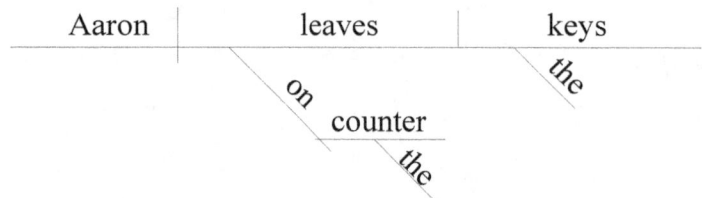

The prepositional phrase *on the counter* is adverbial because it tells us where the verb *leaves* is taking place. We can then break down *on the counter* into its parts. The preposition *on* is placed on a diagonal line from *leaves*, the word the phrase modifies. The object of the preposition, *counter*, is placed on a horizontal line, creating an arm shape. *The* is placed on a diagonal line from *counter* because it modifies *counter*.

Barack Obama is the president of the United States now.

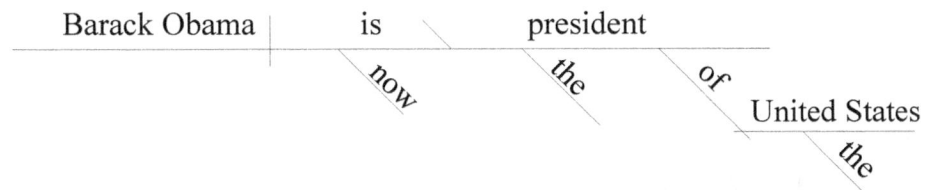

Of the United States is an adjective phrase modifying *president*; it gives us more information, answering the question, "Where is he president?" Therefore, we place the preposition *of* on a diagonal connected to *president*. *United States* completes the "arm" because it is the object of the preposition. *The* modifies *United States*. *Now* is an adverb that modifies the verb *is*, because it answers the question, "When is he president?"

Diagramming Exercises

Your turn! Diagram the following sentences.

1. Sandra is kissing Joseph passionately under the mistletoe.

2. Kate approaches the pool without fear.

3. Applications for college can be quite complicated.

4. Silly children jump on a trampoline without any supervision.

5. At night, teenagers throw wild parties in empty houses.

6. Mimi bakes a chocolate cake for the mysterious man in the street.

7. The surgeon is operating on the valves of the heart with great skill.

8. The surgeon with great skill is operating on the valves of the heart.

9. Many people go to the beach in the month of July.

10. Does Jim have an answer to the difficult question?

11. The plane from Florida is landing at midnight tomorrow.

12. Before the exam, Harriet quietly studies the notes in the hallway.

13. The Trojans wheel the wooden horse of those treacherous Greeks through the gates of the city.

14. Throughout the summer, the Campbells visit the beautiful beaches of New England with friends.

15. Celebrities in the sunny state of California live lavishly in some of the largest homes in the world.

Chapter 4: THE PRONOUN - BASICS

A *pronoun* is a word used to replace a noun.

Examples:
He bought milk.
Julie made *it*.
I am inviting *them* to the party.
You are eating *his* pasta.
Sammy buys *herself* an iced coffee.
Nobody likes *him*.

Pronouns can be categorized into the following groups: *Personal*, *Interrogative*, *Demonstrative*, and *Indefinite*. There are also *Relative* pronouns, but we will cover those in a later chapter.

A *personal pronoun* refers to the 1st person, 2nd person, or 3rd person, singular or plural. Personal pronouns can act as subjects (the personal subjective) or objects (the personal objective), and they take the following forms:

	1st Person Singular	2nd Person Singular	3rd Person Singular	1st Person Plural	2nd Person Plural	3rd Person Plural
Subjective:	I	you	he/she/it	we	you (all)	they
Objective:	me	you	him/her/it	us	you (all)	them

Examples:
I am kicking *him*. (*I* is the subject, *him* is the direct object.)
She is buying *you* candy. (*She* is the subject, *you* is the indirect object.)
They do not like *us*. (*They* is the subject, *us* is the direct object.)
You are baking a pie for *me*. (*You* is the subject, *me* is the object of the preposition.)

Personal pronouns can also be *possessive*, *reflexive*, and *intensive*.

Possessive pronouns answer the question: Whose? (Or, Whose is it?) A possessive pronoun may act as a stand-alone substitute for a possessive noun (Mary's = *hers*), or as a possessive adjective modifying a noun (Mary's book = *her* book). Note that the form changes (from *her* to *hers*, from *my* to *mine*, from *our* to *ours*, etc.) depending on whether the possessive pronoun precedes and modifies another noun or stands alone.

    my, mine
    your, yours (singular you)
    his, her, hers, its
    our, ours

your, yours (plural you – "you all")
their, theirs

Examples:
I told you not to touch *my* books! (Whose books? – *my* books)
Sam just went swimming, so *his* hair is wet. (Whose hair? – *his* hair)
Hurry! *Your* meeting is in five minutes. (Whose meeting? – *your* meeting)
Whose car did he drive? He drove *mine*. (Whose car? – *mine*)

In the first three examples, the pronoun directly modifies the noun that follows it: *my* books, *his* hair, *your* meeting. In the fourth sentence, *mine* stands alone.

Example:
This car is newer than *your* car.
This car is newer than *yours*.

Exercise 1:

Underline the possessive pronoun(s) in the following sentences.

1. His brother is a brilliant student.

2. I am going on a date with her best friend.

3. That house is theirs.

4. Your dress is gorgeous!

5. I love everything about pizza, especially its aroma.

6. This ring is mine, not yours.

7. They are washing my car with their buddies.

Exercise 2:

Use each of following possessive pronouns in an original sentence.

1. my

2. hers

3. their

4. yours

5. your

6. ours

The following pronoun forms can be used *intensively* or *reflexively*:
- myself
- yourself
- himself, herself, itself
- ourselves
- yourselves
- themselves

Reflexive pronouns are used when the subject acts on itself.

Examples:
- I hurt *myself*.
- Make *yourself* some lunch.
- Steven drove *himself* to school.
- The rabid raccoon bit *itself*.
- You may read to *yourselves* quietly.
- Michael and Sarah dressed *themselves* for their first day of kindergarten.

Intensive pronouns emphasize or strengthen the subject.

Examples:
- The boy *himself* saw the robber.
- The girls went door-to-door *themselves*.
- I *myself* broke the doorknob.
- The author *herself* is at the bookstore.
- The president *himself* is coming to Andover.

Exercise 3:

For each pronoun, write two sentences, one using the pronoun reflexively and one using the pronoun intensively.

1. himself

2. myself

3. ourselves

4. yourself

5. themselves

An *interrogative pronoun* introduces a question that requires more than a yes or no answer. The interrogative pronouns are:
> who
> whom
> whose
> which
> what

Who, *which*, and *what* act as subjects.

Examples:
> *Who* is that man?
> *What* are you doing tonight?
> *Which* book is he reading?

Whom acts as an object.

Examples:
> *Whom* are you taking to the dance? (Direct object)
> *To whom* did I give my pencil? (Indirect object)

Whose acts as a possessive.

Example:
> *Whose* chair is that?

Exercise 4:

Write an original question with each interrogative pronoun.

1. who

2. what

3. which

4. whom

5. whose

Like the demonstrative adjective you learned about in Chapter 2, the *demonstrative pronoun* answers the question "Which?" It specifies a particular person or thing. The demonstrative pronouns are:
>this
>that
>these
>those

"This" and "these" refer to objects close to the speaker, while "that" and "those" refer to objects further away from the speaker. Whereas the demonstrative adjective modifies a noun (*this* apple, *those* bananas), the demonstrative pronoun stands alone.

Examples:
>*This* is delicious!
>*Those* do not belong to you.
>Ginny brought *these* to the house yesterday.
>I can take *that* from you.

Exercise 5:

Underline the demonstrative(s) in each sentence and indicate whether they are adjectives or pronouns.

1. I really want that puppy.

2. These cookies have nuts in them.

3. Those are my favorite colors.

4. This party is fantastic!

5. This is a fantastic party!

6. She wants this dress and these shoes.

7. That is truly unbelievable.

8. I never wear this.

9. Kendra is putting all those eggs in this basket.

10. I prefer these cookies to those.

Generally, the noun a pronoun is replacing has already been used. The noun to which the pronoun refers is called its *antecedent*. Personal pronouns must agree with their antecedents in person (1st person, 2nd person or 3rd person), number (singular or plural) and gender (masculine, feminine, or neuter—him vs. her vs. it). A pronoun can also replace another pronoun.

Examples:
> Ben went to the store. *He* bought milk.
> → *He* replaces the noun *Ben*. The context makes it very clear that *he* refers to Ben. *He* agrees with *Ben*: both are 3rd person, singular, and masculine.
>
> The twins are my friends. I invited *them* to the sleepover.
> →*Them* replaces *the twins*. This is very clear from the context. *Them* agrees with *the twins*: both are 3rd person and plural. Whether these particular twins are masculine or feminine is irrelevant; *them* applies to both masculine and feminine (and neuter, though our twins probably aren't neuter) antecedents.

Indefinite pronouns refer imprecisely, or indefinitely, to people, places, things, or ideas. The antecedent is either unknown or simply not expressed.

All	Either	Much	Somebody
Another	Everybody	Neither	Someone
Any	Everyone	Nobody	Something
Anybody	Everything	None	Whatever
Anyone	Few	No one	Whichever
Anything	Many	One	Whoever
Both	More	Several	Whomever
Each	Most	Some	

Examples:
> *Nobody* expected the teacher to throw a pop quiz.
> *Anyone* can come to the party.
> *Whoever* hit that home run is very strong.
> I could eat *anything* right now.
> The ferocious dog bit *both* of the kittens.
> I heard *somebody* call for help.

Always be careful determining whether an indefinite pronoun is singular or plural. For instance, the pronouns *all, most, none,* and *some* can go either way! In these cases, the pronoun takes the number (singular or plural) of the object of the preposition that follows. The verb must agree with the number.

Examples:
> *Some* of the students prefer math to science. (Notice how *some* is plural in this case because *student*s is plural; therefore, the verb *prefer* takes the plural form.)
> *Some* of the money remains unspent. (Notice how *some* is singular in this case because *money* is singular, so the verb *remains* takes the singular form.)

A pronoun sometimes replaces another pronoun. In this case, you must understand whether an indefinite is singular or plural, because your pronouns must agree!

Examples:
> Of the kids in my family, *most* eat their cereal without milk. (*Most* is a plural pronoun, so we use another plural pronoun, *their*, to act as the possessive.)
> If *someone* wants to go to a good college, he or she must work hard in school. (*Someone* is a singular pronoun, so we use the singular pronouns *he or she* to replace it.)
> *Everyone* must hand in his or her homework. (*Everyone* is a singular pronoun, so we use the singular pronouns *his or her* to replace it in the possessive form.)

It is also important to note that many pronouns may function as adjectives, in which case they should be properly categorized as adjectives.

Examples:
> Pronoun: *Several* fell while trying to climb over the slick wall. (In this case, *several* stands on its own, so it is a pronoun.)
> Adjective: *Several Boy Scouts* fell while trying to climb over the slick wall. (In this case, *several* modifies *Boy Scouts*, so it is an adjective.)
> Pronoun: I like *most* of the kids in my class. (In this case, *most* stands on its own, so it is a pronoun.)
> Adjective: I like *most* kids. (In this case, *most* modifies *kids*, so it is an adjective.)

Exercise 6:

For each indefinite word, write two sentences, one using it as a pronoun and one using it as an adjective.

1. Another

2. Neither

3. More

4. Each

5. Much

6. Many

7. Any

Exercise 7:

Identify the types of pronouns used in the following sentences. If a pronoun is personal, identify whether it is subjective, objective or possessive.

1. Gretchen woke herself up for school at 6:30 a.m.
2. To whom are you referring?
3. Put all of the blame on him.
4. Would anybody like to see a movie?
5. In my opinion, red cars look better than blue ones.
6. That, some would say, is intolerable.
7. He did not know that somebody was approaching.
8. Mine are better than yours.
9. John knew them better than anyone.
10. Sheila scored the basket herself.
11. Whose keys are those?
12. Several of the children dressed as witches on Halloween.
13. Someone on the school board leaked information about the closed session to the press.
14. When the cat saw itself in the mirror, it became very frightened.
15. Those documents are mine! Do not touch them!

Exercise 8:

Replaced the underlined word, phrase, or blank with a pronoun, and identify what type of pronoun you are utilizing.

1. Is Johnny speaking with <u>Josephine</u>?
2. Though <u>Sam</u> originally had doubted Pamela, Sam quickly began to trust <u>Pamela</u>.
3. Did Greg throw away <u>Greg's</u> old test papers?
4. Time, <u>Hector</u> argues, is the fourth dimension.
5. When <u>the watch</u> disappeared, neither <u>Jay nor Peter</u> noticed.
6. Margaret asked <u>Jim</u> where it was that she was to drop off <u>Margaret's</u> forms.

7. Is <u>my iPod</u> in your trunk?

8. _____ is knocking at my door?

9. Victoria _____ won the race.

10. _____ of the protesters were wearing scarves.

11. _____ of the protesters was wearing a scarf.

12. _____ of the protesters was wearing a scarf?

13. _____ kind of animal is this?

14. John congratulated <u>John</u> when he won the prize.

15. Is that pen <u>my pen</u>?

Diagramming

Now that you've mastered pronouns, it's time to apply them to your sentence diagramming. The structure of the sentences in this chapter's diagramming is identical to the structure of the sentences you've been working on in previous chapters. The only difference is that pronouns will start to replace other nouns. This means that you must be very aware of each pronoun's role in the sentence: Is it the subject? The direct object? The indirect object? The object of a preposition? Or is it serving as an adjective? You need to determine this in order to diagram the sentence correctly.

Diagramming Exercises

Diagram the following sentences.

1. I am running.

2. Does she need help?

3. He is her friend.

4. You really want that.

5. You really want that jacket.

6. Wanda wants both.

7. Wanda wants both kinds of cake.

8. Is that man actually our new teacher?

9. You like his sister very much.

10. I am going to the new cafe around the corner with your big brother.

11. In the cozy corner, they are reading books aloud to us.

12. I am willingly lending them your car for the rest of their vacation.

CHAPTER 5: MORE ABOUT VERBS

In Chapters 1 and 2, you learned some verb basics: action and linking, transitive and intransitive, and the present and present-progressive tenses. Now you will learn to express more information through your verbs. You can make clear when the verb is taking place, who is performing the verb, or on whom it is being performed. You can tell someone to perform a verb, or you can express verbs that haven't actually taken place but could at some point.

Sometimes a verb consists of multiple words, collectively referred to as a *verb phrase*. This verb phrase consists of the main verb plus one or more *helping verbs* to convey its meaning. These helping verbs allow us to convey different tenses, voices, and moods. Some common helping verbs are:

do	has	can (or may) have
did	had	could (or would, or should) be
does	can	could (or would, or should) have
am	may	will (or shall) have been
are	will (or shall) be	might have
is	will (or shall) have	might have been
was	has (or had) been	must have
were	can (or may) be	must have been
have		

In the following examples, verb phrases are underlined, and helping verbs are italicized.

Examples:
Katie *is* traveling to Vietnam this summer.
You *should have* anticipated losing your work by exiting without saving.
Should you *be* late, we *will* leave without you.
It *must have been* raining outside when the phone rang.
It *must have* been rainy this morning.
Leroy *has* trained his parrot to sing.
It *might have* been useful to save the document before you closed the program.
He *must have been* run out of town by the police.

* Note that in the fourth sentence, *been* is part of the helping verb, while *raining* is the main verb. However, in the sentence that follows, *been* is the main (linking) verb, and is followed by the adjective *rainy*. Likewise, in the seventh sentence, *been* is the main (linking) verb, but in the last example, *been* is part of the helping verb, while *run* is the main (action) verb.

Exercise 1:

Underline all the helping verbs in the following sentences and circle the verb that is being helped.

1. It might have been wise to work hard in high school.

2. You should have foreseen having your finger injured after having placed it under the lawn mower.

3. I have never seen such motivation in a child.

4. To persist may not necessarily be to prevail.

5. You could have saved money by switching to Geico.

6. Bobbie may still catch the train if he leaves now.

7. Had you attended college, you might be making more money now.

8. If you weren't so unsure of yourself, you might be more willing to try new things.

9. Catherine could not understand why Robert didn't find her attractive.

10. Alex had shown up late to work too many times, so his boss fired him.

11. If I had used the copier, I might have saved much time.

12. You should have chosen the apple since you are very hungry.

13. What could have possibly caused the problem?

14. He could have been a scientist if he had wanted to; she could not.

15. They were celebrating Thanksgiving with a large feast.

Now that we have covered all the basics of verbs, we can further explore their usage. All action verbs have a voice, a tense, and a mood, all of which further describe the role of the verb in the sentence and how it works with nouns to create a complete thought.

Recall that the *tense* of an action verb distinguishes the time at which the action was, is, or will be completed. There are three basic tenses (what we will call "simple tenses") in English: present, past, and future.

Present Tense
     The simple present tense, which you learned previously, describes an action that is occurring now, in the present, or makes a general statement about something that occurs or exists in the present.

Examples:
     He *enjoys* swimming.
     The social studies teacher also *coaches* soccer.
     The refrigerator *keeps* food cold.
     Conan O'Brien *tells* funny jokes.

Past Tense
     The simple past tense describes an action that has already taken place and has since been concluded, or makes a statement about such an action. Verbs in the past tense usually end in –ed, with the exception of irregular verbs.

Examples:

I *watched* the movie on Tuesday.
All of the students *failed* the test.
Joe's mother *cooked* dinner on the stove.
The cat *slept* all day long.

In a question, the past may be indicated using the helping verb "to do." In past centuries, this construction was also used in statements ("She did go to Persia"). This usage has become rare except to emphasize an action, often in the face of doubt ("I thought he avoided combat." "No, he did serve in Vietnam," or "She did so like his courtly manner.")

Examples:

Did you *go* to the movies yesterday? (Yes, I *went* with Maria.)
Did you *study* for the science test? (Yes, I *studied* last night.)

Future Tense
The simple future tense describes an action that will occur sometime in the future or to make a statement about an action. The future tense is formed by attaching the helping verbs "will" or "shall" to a main verb.

*The usage of *shall* and *will* is a little bit complex. *Shall* is sometimes used in the first person simply to describe future events, as in, "I shall eat breakfast now." However, *shall* can be used in the second and third person to imply that the subject's wishes have not been considered, as in the command, "You shall not eat any dessert," or the threat, "He shall regret his actions." The distinction can be fuzzy, and the use of *shall* is becoming more and more formal. Therefore, we will mostly use *will* to indicate the future, with some colloquial exceptions such as, "Shall we dance?"

Examples:
This fall, I *will take* the SAT.
He *will take* out his trash on Friday.
The milk *will spoil* in two weeks.
The battery *will die* after three hours.

Exercise 2:

Identify in each of the following sentences whether the verb is simple present, past, or future tense.

1. I will drive my sister to school tomorrow.

2. Did you go to the store yesterday?

3. I look forward to traveling to Boston this weekend.

4. Jessica asked for a laptop for her next birthday.

5. Shall we go to lunch tomorrow?

6. My eyes itch in the springtime due to allergies.

7. This exercise helps you distinguish tenses in English.

8. I need to go to bed now.

9. Paul Revere's house will be open from 9:30 a.m. to 4:30 p.m. in September.

10. My family traveled to Italy last summer.

In addition to the simple form, each of the three tenses introduced above also has a *progressive* form, a *perfect* form, and a *perfect progressive* form.

A *progressive* form of a verb indicates an ongoing or continuous action.

You have already learned the *present progressive* form, which describes an ongoing action that continues to be carried out as the speaker speaks. It is formed by using *am/is/are* with the verb form ending in *–ing*. This is called the present participle, which we will discuss in greater detail later.

Examples:
   The dog *is barking* at the cat.
   Sophie *is driving* to work right now.

The *past progressive* describes an action in the past that was ongoing when another action took place. It is formed by using *was/were* with the present participle.

Examples:
   The birds *were singing* yesterday morning when I woke up.
   I *was sitting* in my office when the burglar broke in.

The *future progressive* describes an ongoing action that will take place sometime in the future. It is formed by using *shall be* or *will be* with the present participle.

Examples:
   I *shall be traveling* to New Hampshire this weekend.
   Sam *will be watching* television on Saturday night.

Exercise 3:

Identify the tense of each of the verbs in the following sentences.

1. I will be traveling to California later this summer.

2. The cat was sitting on the windowsill waiting to be let in.

3. You will be cooking dinner tomorrow at 6:00 p.m.

4. The laptop is running on a very low battery.

5. You are driving me insane!

6. The United States will be electing its next president in three years.

7. That man was running in the marathon yesterday.

8. Henry is taking preventive measures against the swine flu.

9. Henry's sister, Lucy, was laughing at his precautions.

10. Lucy will be suffering from the swine flu next month.

Exercise 4:

Write three sentences for each verb: one using the present progressive, one using the past progressive, and one using the future progressive.

1. walk

2. try

3. bake

The *perfect* form of a verb indicates an action that takes place at an unspecified time. The action may be continuing, or it may be completed.

The *present perfect* describes an action that started in the past and is ongoing (learning or growth, for example), or an action that was completed at an indefinite time in the past. It is formed by using *has* or *have* with the verb form ending in *-ed* (except irregulars).

Examples:
>He *has studied* Latin for three years.
>The teacher *has* never *failed* a student before.
>I *have eaten* seven ice cream sundaes today.

The *past perfect* describes an action happening at an indefinite time in the past that preceded another action that also took place in the past (generally the simple past). It is formed by using *had* with the verb form ending in *-ed* (except irregulars).

Examples:
>I *had studied* Spanish before my family moved to Argentina.
>Dan *had* never *visited* Europe until his company sent him to France.
>Because I *had eaten* so much ice cream, my jeans did not fit.

The *future perfect* describes an action that will happen in the future before another action. It is formed by using *will have* with the verb form ending in *-ed* (except irregulars).

Examples:
>Sue *will have cooked* dinner by the time Joe comes home.
>By the time I turn 18, I *will have graduated* from high school.

Exercise 5:

Identify the tense of each of the verbs in the following sentences.

1. The Smiths have lived in that house for five years now.
2. I had not finished the chapter when we discussed it in class.
3. Jimmy has seen three solar eclipses in his lifetime.
4. He will have studied organic chemistry before he graduates from high school.
5. They had never traveled to Czechoslovakia until last March.
6. We will have eaten all the steak by the time you get home from work.
7. I have never met anyone who likes horses as much as Sally does.
8. Sally had ridden horses her whole life until she fell from one and broke her leg.
9. She will have used crutches for three months before she will be able to walk unaided.
10. Have you ever seen a shark?

Exercise 6:

Write three sentences for each verb: one using the present perfect, one using the past perfect, and one using the future perfect.

1. live

2. explore

3. learn

A *perfect progressive* form of a verb indicates an ongoing action that will be completed at a point in time.

The *present perfect progressive* describes an action that started in the past, continues in the present, and may continue in the future. It is formed by using *has been* or *have been* with the verb form ending in -ing.

Examples:
>I *have been studying* for five hours now!
>The company *has been giving* away large bonuses recently.

The *past perfect progressive* describes an ongoing action completely in the past that was finished before some other action. It is formed by using *had been* with the verb form ending in -ing.

Examples:
>Joe *had been working* for Google for five years before he was laid off.
>The phone *had been ringing* for two minutes when I picked it up.

The *future perfect progressive* describes an ongoing action in the future that will be completed before some specified time. It is formed by using *will have been* with the verb form ending in -ing. Sometimes *is/are going to have been* can also be used.

Examples:
>By the time Charlie graduates, he *will have been studying* Spanish for more than three years!
>I *will have been living* in Andover for 20 years come this September.

Exercise 7:

Identify the tense of each of the main verbs in the following sentences.

1. The diver has been down there for more than half an hour!
2. We will have been driving for eight hours by the time we reach Canada.
3. The employees will have been eating for more than an hour before the CEO joins them.
4. I had only been waiting for ten minutes when Teddy arrived.
5. How long have you been wishing to be a professional musician?
6. How long had you been playing the violin before you decided to quit?
7. Loretta has been giving money to the Salvation Army all her life.
8. At 5:00 a.m., Sammy will have been partying for more than seven hours!
9. The roses had been growing wild before I cut them back.
10. Next month, Jim will have been working in the financial aid office for 10 years.

Exercise 8:

Write three sentences for each verb: one using the present perfect progressive, one using the past perfect progressive, and one using the future perfect progressive.

1. build

2. garden

3. look

Exercise 9:

Identify the tense of the main verbs in the following sentences. They may be any of the 12 tenses introduced in this chapter. Here are your options:

(Simple) Present	(Simple) Past	(Simple) Future
Present Progressive	Past Progressive	Future Progressive
Present Perfect	Past Perfect	Future Perfect
Present Perfect Progressive	Past Perfect Progressive	Future Perfect Progressive

1. She had eaten all her spaghetti by the time he served himself.

2. Harrison will have read 15 books before the summer is over.

3. Maria has been looking for a prom dress since November.

4. Next Wednesday, I will have been working on my novel for four months.

5. Sheila is making a tropical smoothie in the blender.

6. Louise had been waiting for her date for two hours before she finally went home.

7. Olivia will study mathematics at a prestigious university.

8. You were reading the newspaper when I came home.

9. The plane will be landing in a few hours.

10. Alan has driven on the highway many times.

11. Joan greets me on the sidewalk.

12. Monica slept for eight hours last night.

13. Christopher had been painting all morning when a mysterious visitor arrived.

14. His father will be working for a new company in the upcoming months.

15. When she dies, my grandmother will have lived a good life.

16. Charlie has asked four different girls to prom.

17. Larry has been living in New England for 25 years.

18. Many people are waiting on line for tickets.

19. If we shop for one more hour, we will have been shopping half the day!

20. The children were playing baseball in the street when the car drove by.

21. Alana had run five miles before she started feeling dizzy.

22. I do homework for several hours each day.

23. He moved to China at the age of nine.

24. My mother will plant vegetables in her garden this summer.

A verb's *voice* refers to how the verb answers the question: Who is doing what to whom? In other words, the verb's voice expresses how the verb is acting on the subject. An action verb can be either *active* or *passive*.

The *active voice* is used to describe a sentence in which the subject executes the action expressed in the verb. If there is a direct object, it receives this action.

Examples:
> The cat is pouncing.
> The boy ate all of his ice cream.
> The girl reads many books.
> I will run to the end of the block.

The *passive voice* is used when the subject is the recipient of the action expressed in the verb. Often, it is used to emphasize this recipient. There is never a direct object in a passive-voice sentence. In fact, the noun that might function as the direct object in an active sentence becomes the subject in a passive sentence.

Examples:
> All the ice cream was eaten by one boy.
> *Harry Potter* was written by J. K. Rowling.
> The house was finished.
> Dinner is being made as we speak.

In many passive sentences, the prepositional phrase "*by* ..." describes who or what is/was actually doing the action (the equivalent of a subject in an active-voice sentence). Therefore, it is fairly easy to change a passive sentence to an active one by simply switching around the word order.

Examples:

Passive		Active
All the ice cream was eaten by one boy.	→	The boy ate all the ice cream.
Harry Potter was written by J. K. Rowling.	→	J. K. Rowling wrote *Harry Potter*.
The house was finished.	→	They finished the house.

In the last sentence, since the subject was not provided in a prepositional phrase, we have to substitute a subject of our choosing (we chose *they*). As you can see, active sentences are much clearer and easier to read than passive sentences, and in your writing you should use the active voice as much as possible.

Exercise 10:

Identify which of the following sentences are passive and which are active. For all of the passive sentences, rearrange the words to create an active sentence with the same meaning. You may have to supply your own subject.

1. They drank gallons of Coca-Cola at the barbeque.
2. Dozens of hot dogs were consumed as well.
3. This country was founded by Pilgrims.
4. By the time his parents returned, the baby had written all over the walls with pink crayon.
5. Our team was crushed by a larger and more athletic one.
6. The flight from India passed over California three hours ago.
7. The missing child had been found by a lumberjack from a neighboring town.
8. The man was employed by a large investment firm in New York.
9. You were studying the history of China last term.
10. A few years ago, Stephen King, the author of numerous best sellers, was struck by a car.
11. The papers were lost by one of the summer interns.
12. Wite-Out fluid had been spilled all over the table by the teacher.
13. He taught us the history of the American people.
14. We were tested on all the new material.
15. Thousands of cornstalks were flattened by the tornado.
16. The hot chocolate was ordered without whipped cream.
17. Penelope was drawing a self-portrait in charcoal during her art class.
18. The coat rack had been broken by my dog before I returned home.
19. The trees were crushed by high winds during the thunderstorm.

20. I threw the dirty T-shirt into the laundry basket in my bedroom.

21. My silly cat had been jumping all over the apartment while I was out.

22. The island's people had been devastated by a tidal wave.

23. The store was robbed by a masked man.

24. Sheila will buy three dozen eggs and 5 pounds of potatoes for her famous frittatas.

25. The floor was vacuumed yesterday by the cleaning crew.

26. I slept for 12 hours after the New Year's Eve party last week.

27. The rowdy party was broken up by the police.

28. *Star Wars* was written, directed, and produced by George Lucas.

The *mood* of a verb denotes the attitude that the speaker assumes toward the verb's action. The most common mood, the *indicative*, describes an action that is regarded as undisputed fact or truth. It is important to realize that the action does not have to be true in real life, only regarded as truth in the sentence.

Examples:
> Mr. Beaven is a tutor in Andover, Massachusetts.
> The pig flew over Italy. (Although this sentence is not true, notice how the verb asserts the fact as truth. If the sentence had read: "The pig *might have flown* over Italy," then the verb would *not* be indicative.)

The *subjunctive* mood describes an action that may be uncertain, hoped for, disputable, dependent on another action or condition, or simply contrary to fact.

Examples:
> If it *should rain* tomorrow, I *would carry* an umbrella.
> The pig *might have flown* over Italy.
> If it *had snowed* yesterday, I *would have made* a snowman.

Lastly, the *imperative* mood is used to express a command. It is sometimes accompanied by an address to a specific person, or the subject "you" is implied. The next chapter will cover nouns of direct address.

Examples:
> Rachael, *fetch* me the axe.
> *Don't sit* on my bed!

Diagramming

There is no new diagramming for this chapter. The verbs you've learned are diagrammed just like the most basic verbs. Helping verbs stay with their main verbs; verb phrases stay together.

Examples:

I will study.

```
    I    |    will study
_____|_____
```

I have been studying.

```
    I    |    have been studying
_____|_____
```

Chapter 6: CONJUNCTIONS, INTERJECTIONS, AND DIRECT ADDRESS

Conjunctions

Conjunctions are words used to join words or phrases together, while indicating their relationship.

Examples:
    Mary-Kate ***and*** Ashley Olsen have starred in numerous films.
    She is ***neither*** stupid ***nor*** unattractive.
    I eat chocolate cake every day ***but*** I don't gain weight.

There are three types of conjunctions: *coordinating*, *correlative*, and *subordinating*. We will cover subordinating conjunctions when we introduce subordinate clauses in a later chapter.

Coordinating conjunctions join two sentence elements, whether they are subjects, objects, phrases, etc.

The coordinating conjunctions are:
    for   and   not   but   or   yet   so   (*Remember with the acronym FANBOYS)

Multiple subjects connected by a conjunction are called a *compound subject*.

Examples: Jack *and* Jill went up the hill.
                Jose *and* I are in the same class.

* Note that compound subjects may take a singular or a plural form of the verb. Compound subjects connected by *and* take the plural form of the verb. Those connected by *or* agree with the noun immediately preceding the verb.

Examples: The soccer ball *and* Maradona jersey **make** a good raffle item for the charity auction.
                The soccer ball *or* Maradona jersey **makes** a good raffle item.
                The mascot *or* the cheerleaders **are** going to entertain before the game.
                The cheerleaders *or* the mascot **is** going to entertain before the game.

Multiple direct objects connected by a conjunction are called a *compound direct object*. The same rule applies to indirect objects.

Examples: Kendra writes poems *and* short stories.
                The man sold my uncle *and* aunt a new sofa.

Multiple predicate adjectives connected by a conjunction are called a *compound predicate adjective*. The same rule applies to predicate nominatives.

Examples: Frankie is handsome *but* stupid.
   Francine is a banker, *not* an accountant.

Multiple prepositional phrases connected by a conjunction are called a *compound prepositional phrase*.

Example: Is he from Houston *or* Dallas?

Multiple ideas, or *independent clauses* (which we will learn more about in a later chapter), connected by one or more conjunctions constitute a *compound sentence*.

Example: Trisha went to the frat party, *but* her roommate stayed in the dorm.

Knowing the names *compound subject*, *compound object*, etc. is not as important as recognizing that a coordinating conjunction joins together two of the same type of word, phrase, or other element.

Correlative conjunctions are always used in pairs. Some correlative conjunctions are:

   both...and   whether...or   not only...but also
   either...or   neither...nor

Examples:
   Neither the parents *nor* the students approved of the new teacher.
   Both Eliza *and* her sister are cheerleaders.
   Mira will cook *either* chicken *or* tofu for dinner.

Like coordinating conjunctions, correlative conjunctions link two of the same type of sentence element. When they form a compound subject, it may take either the singular or plural form of the verb. *Neither...nor*, *whether...or*, and *either...or* all require the singular form, as they indicate that only one of the subjects – or neither subject – will be performing the action of the verb. *Both...and* requires the plural form, as it means that more than one person, place, thing, or idea is performing the action of the verb.

Examples:
   Either Natasha *or* Elinore **is** going to the prom with Mahmoud.
   Both Tyler *and* Ethan **are** going to run for student council president.

Exercise 1:

Combine the following sentences into one by adding conjunctions where needed.

1. Mr. Thompson is a math teacher at the high school. Mr. Thompson is a soccer coach at the high school.

2. Jonah skied in the Alps over Christmas break. He had a great time.

3. Tom has traveled to England. Tom has never gone to France.

4. The coffee is too hot. I will drink it lukewarm.

5. Tony wants to order shrimp scampi. He wants to order steak as well. He doesn't have room for both.

6. I would eat rice. I would not eat potatoes.

7. We could cook dinner. Alternatively, we could just order takeout from the Chinese restaurant.

8. He needs to study hard for this test. If he does not, he will fail the class.

Exercise 2:

Insert the missing correlative conjunction where appropriate.

1. Either Tom _____ Bobby should take out the garbage before midnight.
2. I do not know _____ to go to class or skip it.
3. Neither Greg _____ Justin graduated from high school.
4. Both Greg _____ Justin will be working as garbagemen.
5. At the barbeque, Alyssa ate not only a hamburger, _____ a hot dog.

Interjections

An *interjection* is generally a word used to express emotion or intense feeling. It usually stands alone and is followed by an exclamation point. An interjection can also be a short phrase used in the same manner. Many expletives, profanities, and obscenities also are used as interjections.

Examples:
    Hooray!
    Hey!
    What?
    Oh!
    Alas!
    Really!
    Ouch!

Holy smokes!
Awesome!
Yuck!
Gosh darn it!
Yikes!

Nouns of Direct Address

A *noun of direct address* is used when someone is being spoken to directly. It is set off by commas and has no grammatical effect on the rest of the sentence.

Examples:
Dad, would you please pass the salt?
What would you like to do, *Sasha*?
Inge, did you watch the new episode last night?

Direct address can also be used with the imperative mood to give a command.

Examples:
Ben, come here this instant!
Eat your vegetables, *Jeff*.
Children, clean your rooms.

Diagramming

Both *coordinating conjunctions* and *correlative conjunctions* are diagrammed by connecting the two joined sentence elements with a dotted line. The conjunction is written along the dotted line.

Example:

Bill and Al will bake either cookies or brownies.

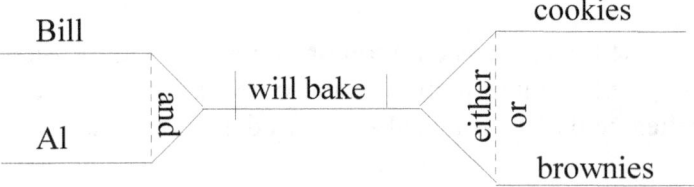

This sentence has a compound subject (*Bill and Al*) and a compound object (*either cookies or brownies*). We join the two subjects with a dotted line and the two direct objects with a dotted line. We also write the conjunction on the line, whether it is coordinating or correlative.

A *compound sentence*, two ideas joined by a conjunction, is diagrammed as though it were two separate sentences, and then a broken, dotted line connects the two sentences' verbs.

Example:

Elizabeth went to the movies, but Patty watched television at home.

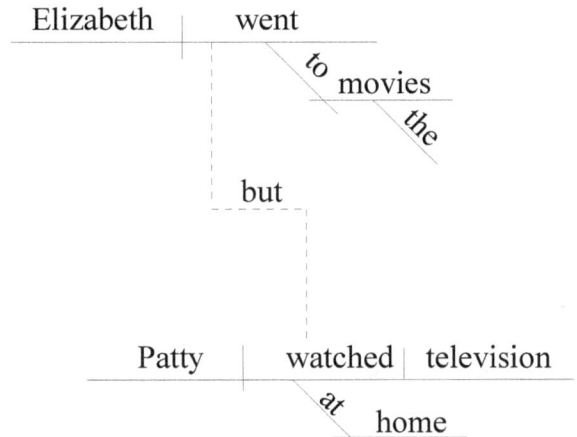

In this sentence, the conjunction *but* joins two separate sentence ideas. Each has its own subject and verb and could stand alone as a sentence: They are two *independent clauses*. We connect the two sentences at their respective verbs with a broken, dotted line, and we place the conjunction on the horizontal portion of that line.

Interjections are diagrammed on their own, separate line above an accompanying sentence.

Example:

Hooray! We won the game!

```
    Hooray


  We | won | game
              \the
```

Hooray is an interjection, not part of the main sentence which accompanies it. However, the interjection and sentence complement each other: *Hooray* adds a strong, emotional tone to the main sentence, while the main sentence explains the reason for the emotion expressed in the interjection.

Nouns of direct address are diagrammed like interjections. Again, they do not alter the grammatical structure of the main sentence.

Example:

Charlie, do you want some pudding?

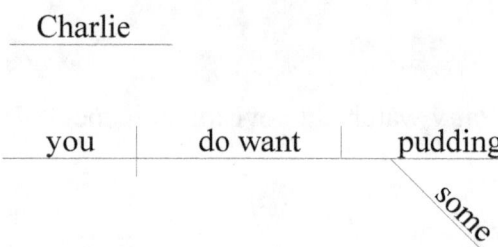

Charlie identifies the person being addressed, but does not affect the sentence's grammatical structure, so it sits apart.

Imperative verbs, whether or not they use a noun of direct address, are diagrammed a special way. Imperatives do not come with an expressed subject, but they all have the unexpressed subject *you*. Therefore, where we would ordinarily diagram a subject, we simply place an *x* to remind us that the subject is unexpressed. If there is a noun of direct address, we still diagram it above the rest of the sentence.

Examples:

Feed the cat!

Eleanor, feed the cat!

Diagramming Exercises:

Diagram the following sentences on your own:

1. Christine is both extremely intelligent and intensely beautiful.

2. Kelly and Kyle are having coffee and cookies on their porch.

3. Neither Mrs. Plunkett nor Mr. Redman buys fancy clothes or is tall and thin.

4. Does this boy live in a city in Texas or in a suburb in California?

5. Either Jimmy or Julia will come through the door and into the room, but the other will not come.

6. They walked for several years through hot deserts and gloomy forests, and they finally came to their homeland.

7. Our team has passion, dedication, and desire, but their team has neither heart nor soul.

8. Every student in the group not only participated in the discussion, but also worked tirelessly and passionately.

9. How many cookies did he eat and from whom did he get them?

CHAPTER 7: VERBALS AND PHRASES

Phrases

A *phrase* is a group of connected words that does **not** contain both a subject and a verb.

Examples:
    on the roof
    loving the dance
    to coexist

You have already learned about one important type of phrase: the prepositional phrase. You have also learned to determine whether a particular prepositional phrase is functioning as an adverb phrase or an adjective phrase.

Now you will learn about a few other types of phrases.

Appositive Phrases

An *appositive* is a noun, pronoun, or group of words that follows another noun or pronoun in order to give more information about it. An *appositive phrase* is composed of the appositive and its modifiers. This may sound confusing, but you probably use appositives all the time without realizing it. Appositives and appositive phrases are usually set apart by a comma or a pair of commas. Note that a name or other proper noun may be the appositive, if preceded by a descriptive phrase; if the name comes first, then the description that follows is an appositive phrase.

Examples:
    My youngest sister, *Nancy*, went to the shore.
    George Bush, *the former president of the United States*, is from Texas. (*President* is the
        appositive noun that renames *George* Bush; *president* and all the words modifying it
        constitute the appositive phrase.)
    I am going to cook chicken parmesan, *my favorite meal*.
    I'm having dinner with my friend *Janelle*.

Exercise 1:

In each sentence, bracket the appositive phrase(s).

1. Mr. Smith, the baker, wakes up at 6 a.m. daily.

2. I would like to be friends with Ashley and Veronica, two very popular girls in our class.

3. My pal Miranda loves going shopping with me.

4. Josh Beckett, tonight's starting pitcher for the Red Sox, has an impressive record.

5. The Oscar-winning actor Sean Penn will be making an appearance.

6. Sophocles, author of many ancient Greek tragedies, died at the age of ninety.

7. Hawaiian senator Daniel Akaka is a member of the Democratic Party.

8. Grammar, a subject typically despised by young students, is easy to learn with this book, an engaging compilation of examples and exercises.

Exercise 2:

Use each noun in apposition in a sentence. You may use other words to modify the noun.

1. cousin

2. athlete

3. Kathryn

4. ice cream

5. pet peeve

6. dog

7. author

8. treasurer

Verbals and Their Phrases

A *verbal* is any form of a verb acting as another part of speech. The three verbals are *participles* (verbal adjectives), *gerunds* (verbal nouns), and *infinitives* (verbal adjectives, verbal nouns, or verbal adverbs).

Examples:
The *swimming* boy was playing "Marco Polo."	Participle → functions as an adjective
Swimming is a fun activity.	Gerund → functions as a noun
I like *to swim*.	Infinitive

We will cover participles and gerunds in this chapter, and we will give infinitives their own chapter later on.

Participles and Participial Phrases

Participles have two tenses: the *present participle*, formed by adding *-ing* to a verb, and the *past participle*, formed by adding *-ed* to the verb (or *-en*, *-t*, etc. in the case of irregular verbs) and using the helping verbs "having" or "having been." Like verbs, participles can be active or passive. We will cover the present active, past active, and past passive participles.

Examples: dance
  Present active participle: *dancing*
  Past active participle: *having danced*
  Past passive participle: *having been danced*

Participles, like adjectives, are used to modify nouns. Though they convey action, they are not verbs. The present participle tells the action a noun is performing, while the past participle is used to describe what a noun has done (active), or what has been done to a noun (passive).

The boy, *dancing* with the girl, blushed.	Present
The boy, *having danced* with the girl, blushed.	Past active
The boy, *having been danced* around the room by the girl, blushed.	Past passive

Participles may or may not take an <u>object</u>.

Examples:
Tony, *singing,* walked to the store.	No object
Tony, *singing* a <u>song</u>, walked to the store.	Direct object
Tony, *singing* <u>me</u> a <u>song</u>, walked to the store.	Direct and indirect objects

The past passive participle often appears before or after the noun it modifies without the helping verbs "having been." Likewise, the present participle may appear on its own in front of the noun it modifies. Sometimes the "having been" may be dropped from a participial phrase as well.

Examples:
  He couldn't wiggle his *frozen* toes.
  The *crumpled* paper bag blew away in the *howling* wind.

He adjusted the *chiming* clock with a *bent* paperclip.
The pot, *blackened* with soot, sat on the *smoldering* campfire.

Exercise 3:

Underline each participle. Determine whether it is present, past active, or past passive.

1. The chef, baking a cake, stirred the frosting.
2. The silenced crowd watched in awe.
3. The boy running by my house waved hello.
4. Having changed her mind, Lara turned and ran the other way.
5. The girl, driving her car, made a wrong turn.
6. Lisa noticed the boy singing a song.
7. John, having eaten half the apple, noticed a wriggling worm inside.
8. Having said goodbye to my friends and family, I boarded the waiting plane.
9. The shimmering comet rose higher into the sky until it was above the mesmerized crowd.
10. The reheated meal was eaten by the girl.
11. Mr. Hobart, teaching a class, called on the girl sitting in the back.

Exercise 4:

Change the following italicized expressions into a participle or participial phrase.

1. the dog *that was barking*
2. the yogurt *that had been frozen*
3. the boy *who is swimming*
4. the star *that was shining*
5. the cat *that is purring*
6. the frog *that was croaking*
7. the store *that had been shuttered*
8. the apple *that had been infested by a worm*
9. the girl *who had eaten ten apple pies*
10. the car *that had been painted red*

Exercise 5:

Complete the sentences with the present or past participle of the verbs below.

Be   Walk   Devastate   Write   Find   Scan   Compose   Chew

1. _____ bad at grammar, I need to use sentence diagrams to help me understand!
2. _____ by brilliant interns, this book is bound to make me smarter.
3. _____ this particular science class too easy, I will soon switch to another.
4. I would hate to find _____ gum under my desk.
5. _____ down the street, I saw the traffic light change to red.
6. _____ by the recent influenza outbreak, the city's population has dwindled.
7. _____ her notes one last time before the test, Kim entered the classroom.
8. This symphony, _____ by Beethoven, is an important work in the history of classical music.

Gerund Phrases

Gerunds, or verbal nouns, are formed by adding *-ing* to a word. They appear similar to participles, but they are used as nouns rather than adjectives. They are able to perform any job that a noun is able to perform (i.e. subject, direct object, predicate nominative, etc.). It helps to think of them as naming an activity or a state of being.

Examples:
    Skiing is an enjoyable winter sport.   Subject
    Sam hates *fighting*.   Direct object
    My favorite activity is *painting*.   Predicate nominative
    Kyla can engage any audience with her *acting*.   Object of a preposition

Gerunds are often modified and may take their own direct objects, adverbs, or predicate nominatives/adjectives. The entire phrase containing a gerund and any modifiers, objects, or predicates is known as the *gerund phrase*.

Examples:
    [*Reading* books] is my favorite way to spend the afternoon. (takes the direct object *books*)
    Lenny hates [*being* dirty]. (takes the predicate adjective *dirty*)
    [His *cheating* on tests] really bothers me. (modified by the possessive pronoun *his* and the
        prepositional phrase *on tests*)
    [*Running* quickly] is a surefire way to win a race. (modified by the adverb *quickly*)

Exercise 6:

In each sentence, underline the gerund and bracket the gerund phrase(s).

1. Pamela enjoys [playing softball].
2. [Eating pizza and ice cream every day] isn't healthy.
3. Charlie evaded punishment by [lying about his misdemeanors].
4. [Watching movies] makes me sleepy.
5. She loves [strolling through the park with her best friends].
6. [Dissecting earthworms] is quite fascinating.
7. [Speaking in Pig Latin] becomes boring very quickly.
8. My baby's constant crying is distressing me.
9. I love [speaking in foreign languages].
10. Winning is quite rewarding.

Exercise 7:

Change each verb into a gerund and use it in a sentence. Vary your sentences!

1. ski

2. run

3. read

4. eat

5. swim

6. play

7. fly

8. contemplate

Exercise 8:

Write sentences using each word in a gerund phrase. Remember that a noun does not have to be the direct object of a gerund.

Example: Paris → Walking through the streets of Paris fills me with joy.

1. dictionary

2. computer

3. carelessly

4. cell phone

5. quickly

6. shower

Exercise 9:

Follow the directions of the previous exercise. This time, you must use the gerund phrase in the role provided.

Example: dog, object of a preposition → I get my daily exercise by walking my dog.

1. gum, subject

2. cookies, direct object

3. kitchen, predicate nominative

4. slowly, subject

5. shoes, object of a preposition

6. garbage, direct object

Gerunds and participles can often be mistaken for one another. Let's look at some examples of each.

Examples:
    The *dancing* bear is very big.
    → *Dancing* is modifying the noun *bear* here just like an adjective. Therefore, *dancing* is a participle.

    Dancing is a fun and healthy form of exercise.
    → Here, *dancing* is functioning as a noun; it is the subject of the sentence. Therefore, *dancing* is a gerund.

    Look at those *fighting* squirrels!
    → *Fighting* is modifying the noun *squirrels*, and is therefore a participle.

    Fighting squirrels all day really tires out my dog Rex.
    → You may be tempted to say that *fighting* is modifying *squirrels* as it did in the previous example. But here *fighting* is functioning as a noun, the subject of the sentence, so it is a gerund, with *squirrels* as its direct object. To put it another way, in the first example, the squirrels are doing the fighting. In the second, Rex is doing the fighting and the squirrels are **what** he is fighting.

*If you are not sure whether something is a gerund or participle, try adding the words "the act of" in front of it. A sentence with a gerund will still make sense:

    [The act of] dancing is a fun and healthy form of exercise.

    [The act of] fighting squirrels all day really drains Nick of energy.

A participle sentence will make NO sense!

    The [the act of] dancing bear is very large.

    Look at those [the act of] fighting squirrels!

Exercise 10:
Underline all gerunds and participles. Then place a G over gerunds and a P over participles.

1. Swimming in the pond, John became covered in muck.
2. After the ringing of the doorbell quieted, Mark answered.

3. John witnessed Queen Elizabeth's crowning.

4. Having been embarrassed by her apparent lack of preparation, Michelle recovered by answering the next three questions correctly.

5. When I was a kid, my favorite playground activity was swinging.

6. Having seen the movie already, Brian anticipated the twist at the end.

7. Reveling in his glory, Sam celebrated his winning the race.

8. Thinking too hard can cause headaches!

9. Having written numerous best sellers, Jim was accosted by people asking him for publishing advice.

10. Young girls often enjoy playing with dolls.

Exercise 11:

Change each verb into a verbal of your choice and write a sentence using it. Note whether you used it as a gerund or a participle. If two verbs are given, you may use both a participle and a gerund if you wish.

Example: call, see
> The hiker, having seen someone in the distance, got his attention by calling for help.
> (having seen = participle, calling = gerund)

1. skate

2. eat

3. exercise

4. hear

5. read, write

6. win, run

7. fly, bite

8. look, find

Diagramming

Appositive phrases are diagrammed by placing the appositive within parentheses next to the word it modifies and by following all rules about modifiers.

Example: Usain Bolt, the fastest man on Earth, won the race.

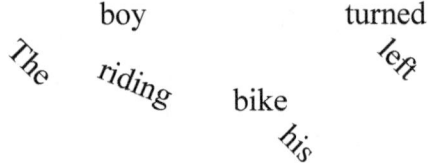

    Usain Bolt is the subject, *won* is the verb, and *race* (modified by *the*) is the direct object. *Man* is in apposition with *Usain Bolt*, so we put it in parentheses. *The*, *fastest*, and *on Earth* modify the appositive *man*, so we follow the same diagramming rules regarding modifiers.

Participial phrases are diagrammed by connecting a horizontal line to the main sentence line with a diagonal line underneath the word that is modified by the participial phrase. The participle is placed diagonally on the figure. Any objects are diagrammed as if the participle were a verb.

Example: The boy, riding his bike, turned left.

    Boy, modified by *the*, is the subject of the sentence, and *turned* is the verb, modified by the adverb *left*. We now are left with the participial phrase *riding his bike*. Participle phrases are adjectives; this one modifies *boy*. *Riding* is the actual participle, and it takes the direct object *bike*. *His* modifies *bike*.

Gerunds are diagrammed as follows:

Example: Swimming in pools is enjoyable.

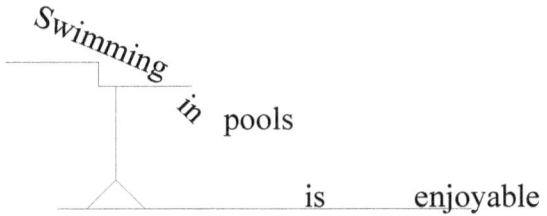

You already know that *is* is the sentence's verb, and *enjoyable* is a predicate adjective. Here's the new part: The gerund *swimming* is the subject of the sentence, so we place it above the horizontal sentence line on a step-like structure. *In pools* is a prepositional phrase that tells us more about the verbal part of the gerund (What kind of swimming? Swimming in pools), so we diagram it like a regular prepositional phrase from the lower (right-hand) portion of the "step."

It is important to be able to distinguish between the verbal and noun-related aspects of a gerund. Also, gerunds are diagrammed slightly differently when they are objects of prepositions. This next example will demonstrate both.

Example:
I am irritated by his telling lies to me.

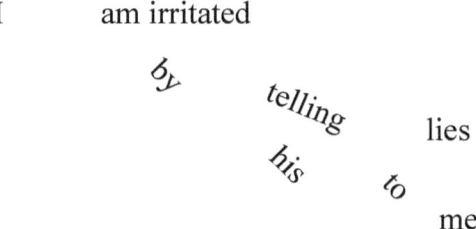

Telling is a gerund functioning as the object of the preposition *by*. Notice that the gerund is still on a step, just like the previous example. However, this gerund, because it is the object of a preposition and comes underneath the main sentence line, is not on top of a vertical structure like *swimming* was in the previous sentence. *Lies* is the gerund's direct object, so we diagram *lies* just as we would any direct object.

Here's where it gets tricky. Gerunds are essentially a hybrid between a noun and a verb. *His* modifies the *noun* part of the gerund. You'd use *his* to modify other nouns: his baseball, his cereal, his shoelace. The adverbial prepositional phrase *to me*, however, describes the *verbal* part of the gerund. You'd use *to me* to modify other verbs: give to me, say to me, describe to me. We place everything modifying the *noun* part of a gerund on the upper portion (left-hand) of the step, and we place everything modifying the *verbal* part of a gerund on the lower portion (right-hand) of the step.

Diagramming Exercises

Diagram the following sentences:

1. Joan, a musician, loves flying with her family.

2. Looking at the passing clouds, I saw the shape of a dragon.

3. An excess of earwax blocked his hearing.

4. I escaped the barking dog by jumping over the fence.

5. Reading well is a very important skill for high school.

6. The girl, crimping her hair, dropped the hot iron onto the floor of her bathroom.

7. Walking around the street on a hot day, I bumped into my neighbor carrying his groceries.

8. Carrying his groceries, I bumped into my neighbor walking around the street on a hot day.

9. Kelly, the woman painting my nails, is telling me a story about gardening.

10. Several people kept gawking at the burning house.

11. Having read the offensive letter written by the CEO angered by the terrible work of his lazy employees, I promptly quit my job.

12. A book, autographed by its famous author, was sitting on the counter.

13. Having been spotted in the crowd by throngs of her adoring fans, the celebrity was surrounded by a circle of guards protecting her safety.

14. Lila, fascinated by studying ancient cultures, visited decaying ruins throughout South America.

15. My extremely lazy son should clean his bedroom without my asking.

16. My being reprimanded for my misdeeds will change my attitude about behaving badly.

Chapter 8: INFINITIVES

The *infinitive* is the basic form of a verb – its "pure" form, apart from any particular subject or tense. It is preceded by the word *to*: for example, *to swim, to learn, to be,* or *to have*. In ordinary usage, it may act as a noun, an adjective, or an adverb.

Examples:

To volunteer for charity is admirable.	Noun
Greg's job – *to clean* his room – took hours.	Adjective (modifies the noun *job*)
The coals were too hot *to touch*.	Adverb (modifies the adjective *hot*)

An *infinitive phrase* is an infinitive and any objects, adverbs, or other modifiers that may apply to it.

Examples:

My friend dared me *to chug my milkshake*.	Takes a direct object
I want *to jump on the trampoline*.	Takes a prepositional phrase
Freddie tried *to explain the concept clearly*.	Takes a direct object and an adverb

Sometimes it is difficult to figure out what part of speech the infinitive phrase represents, especially if it is lengthy or removed from the word it modifies. If you can substitute the word "this" or "that," then it is acting as a noun. If the infinitive phrase answers the question of "Why?" the main verb is performed, then it is acting as an adverb. It is also acting as an adverb if it describes, or modifies an adjective. If it further explains or describes a noun, it is acting as an adjective.

Examples:

He studied Chinese all through college *to improve his chances of joining the foreign service*.
    (Adverb, because it answers the question, "Why did he study?")
To live a life of quiet contemplation was their only wish. (Noun, because you can logically state, "This was their only wish.")
I had hoped *to see him succeed*. (Note that there are two infinitives in this phrase, a noun phrase that acts as the direct object of the verb *hoped*. Within the noun phrase there is a second infinitive, *(to) succeed*, which acts as the object of the first infinitive, *to see*. *Him* is the subject of the second infinitive, *(to) succeed*.)

The infinitive frequently appears after the main <u>verb</u> to complete its meaning. This is true in the third example above, and is especially common following verbs such as *hope, try, want, dare, convince, prefer, like, go,* and *learn*. The infinitive is then acting like a noun – specifically, a direct object – because it answers the question "What (received the action of the verb)?"

Examples:

I <u>want</u> *to win*.
They <u>tried</u> *to persuade* me to run for governor.
We <u>learned</u> *to conjugate* regular verbs in Spanish class this week.
They <u>like</u> *to eat* pizza.

<u>Have</u> you <u>gone</u> *to work out* yet?

*Note that sometimes the word "to" will be omitted. Rather than "Don't you dare to disobey!" people commonly say, "Don't you dare disobey!" The word "to" will also be omitted after the first infinitive in a series, because it is implied: "He wanted *to retire*, *learn* Italian, and *visit* Italy," instead of "*to retire, to learn...*, and *to visit.*"

An infinitive may also have its own subject. If it does, the subject, along with the infinitive and any modifiers or objects, is known as an *infinitive clause*. (Clauses will be discussed in greater detail in the next chapter.)

Examples:

The boy asked his *mother to make him lunch*.	*mother* is the subject of *to make*
Pedro told *Alexis to lock the door*.	*Alexis* is the subject of *to lock*
I want *Mr. Richardson to be my teacher*.	*Mr. Richardson* is the subject of *to be*

Be careful not to confuse an infinitive with prepositional phrases using the preposition *to*. Prepositional phrases do not contain verbs.

Examples:

I am going *to the store*.	Prepositional phrase
I am going *to buy* milk.	Infinitive
Sam went *to the concert*.	Prepositional phrase
Sam went *to see* his favorite band.	Infinitive

*Note that some helping verbs do not have an infinitive form. These include *will, shall, should, would, ought, may, might, must, can,* and *could*. However, the three most common helping verbs – *to be, to have,* and *to do* – have an infinitive form.

Exercise 1:

Use the following infinitives or infinitive phrases in an original sentence. Try to vary your sentences, using the infinitive as a noun, an adjective, and an adverb.

1. To talk

2. To disagree

3. To eat junk food

4. To make you an offer

5. To hear

6. To be

7. To make his bed

8. To leave

Exercise 2:

Underline each infinitive phrase and determine whether each is functioning as a noun, adjective, or adverb.

1. To be dishonest in school is a problem.
2. It is too hard to chew.
3. The day to begin college had arrived.
4. This urge to pick my nose is overwhelming.
5. She is difficult to resist.
6. I would love to visit the Dead Sea sometime.
7. Ronnie would sacrifice anything to be a rock star.
8. My father put a mousetrap in the garage to capture that pesky rodent.
9. One way to annoy your sister would be to put frogs in her bed.
10. To avoid running into that arrogant football player was the only thing on her mind.
11. To jump out of a plane without a parachute is insane.
12. Knights in medieval times always wore armor in battle to protect themselves.
13. Many people learn to read very early in life, because reading is an important skill to have.
14. To volunteer at a charity is generous, but many people are too busy to help out.
15. I have so many notes to review and old tests to study!
16. I want to go to the zoo, because I love to see all the different animals.
17. The dog was barking loudly, so her owners rushed outside to check on her.
18. Fantasy authors write to interest their readers and create a magical world.

Diagramming

It's time to put your infinitive skills to the test! Infinitive phrases are diagrammed similarly to gerunds; the verb sits on a line parallel to the sentence line, while the *to* sits on a slant.

Examples:
    I want to eat cake.

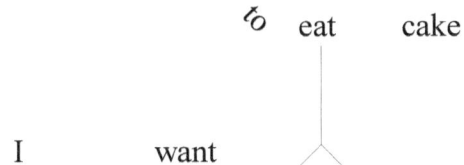

    In this sentence, the infinitive phrase *to eat cake* functions as a noun: specifically, a direct object. Therefore, we diagram the phrase as if it were a direct object after the verb *want*. We put the phrase on a structure much like that for the gerund. *To* is placed on a slant, and the actual verb, *eat* in this case, is put on the horizontal line. This particular infinitive phrase contains a direct object, *cake*. We diagram it next to the verb *eat*, like any other direct object.

    It is still too early to know.

    Here the infinitive is functioning as an adverb modifying the adjective *early*. In such a case, the infinitive is diagrammed below the sentence line, but the basic shape (*to* on a slant, *verb* on the horizontal) stays the same.

Diagramming Exercises

Diagram the following sentences:

1. To be a famous actor is his only goal.

2. I like to jog in this neighborhood before sunset.

3. Wilma decided to give her favorite vintage necklace to her loving granddaughter as a gift.

4. The purpose of this silly example is to teach diagramming infinitives.

5. Be sure to lower the thermostat in the kitchen after dinner.

6. It is much too hot outside to drink coffee, tea, and cocoa.

7. Many of my friends with licenses like to and are allowed to drive their cars to school each day.

8. Our teachers do not let us, their students, put our aching feet on our desks during class.

9. Studying physics makes me want to ram my head against a wall repeatedly.

10. I am unable to assist you further.

11. Patricia, despite her hostile and aggressive manner, wants nothing but to have friends.

12. I have several interesting books for her to read over the course of the year.

13. It was truly unnecessary for you to call me those rude names with my boyfriend standing there.

CHAPTER 9: CLAUSES

A *clause* is a group of words containing a subject and a verb, used as part of a sentence. There are many different types of clauses.

If a clause makes sense on its own (as a sentence), it is known as an *independent clause* or a *main clause*.

Examples:
    Tom is a rather large man.
    The square root of four is two.
    Jason loves eating broccoli.

Every sentence must have a subject and a verb, and sentences with transitive verbs must have a direct object: A sentence that does not is incomplete, or a sentence fragment. While these may be used occasionally for literary effect, they have no place in academic writing or the essay because they do not contribute to clarity of meaning. Conversely, two or more clauses joined together without a conjunction to show their relationship make a run-on sentence. A comma is not a conjunction!

Examples:
    Going to the market. (Fragment: It has no subject)
    Todd needed. (Fragment: The transitive verb *needed* has no direct object)
    He went to the market, she was at work. (Run-on: It lacks a conjunction)

If a clause does not make sense on its own, it is known as a *dependent clause* or a *subordinate clause*, and must be attached to an independent clause.

Examples:
    While I was preparing for work, I packed my computer.
    I saw the tall man *who bumped his head*.
    The phone rang *as soon as I walked in the door*.
    James asked *where he should go*.

Any of these dependent clauses on its own would be a sentence fragment.

*Note that participial phrases and gerund phrases are not clauses because they do not have a subject and a verb.

Exercise 1:

Underline independent clauses once and dependent clauses twice.

1. When you finish reading that book, you should try reading this one.
2. I don't know how warm it is outside.

3. The man who wrote the book died before it was published.

4. Please put away your dishes after you wash them.

5. Walking to the store, the young boy tripped when he stubbed his toe.

There are three types of subordinate clauses: *adverb clauses*, *adjective clauses*, and *noun clauses*.

Adverb Clauses

Subordinate clauses that act as adverbs are called adverb clauses. These clauses answer the same types of questions about verbs that adverbs answer.

Examples:
Peggy goes *wherever her friends go*. (Answers the question: Where does she go?)
Because Rick was too weak, he could not move the heavy stone. (Answers: Why couldn't he move it?)
I will eat dinner *before my friends come over.* (Answers: When will you eat?)
Even though he was a bright student, he was not admitted. (Answers: Why is this unexpected?)
If you exercise daily, you will lose more weight. (Answers: How, or under what circumstances?)
Kathy studied for hours *so that she would get a better grade*. (Answers: Why, or for what purpose?)

The word that introduces an adverb phrase is known as a *subordinating conjunction*. The subordinating conjunction serves to show how the adverb clause relates to the main clause (when, where, how, etc.).

Examples:
I will fall ill *if* I eat too much food.   (Under what circumstances?)
Because I did not study, I failed.   (Why?)
I quit *after* the other boy left.   (When?)

Commonly Used Subordinating Conjunctions:

after	before	provided	though	whenever
although	how	since	unless	where
as	if	so that	until	wherever
as much as	in order that	than	when	while
because				

Because adverb clauses act like regular adverbs, they may also be used to modify adverbs and adjectives. This is usually done by using the subordinating conjunction *than* to make a comparison.

Examples:
Next time you work, go over the paper more carefully *than* you did last time.

(adverb phrase modifying the adverb *carefully*)
The house is bigger *than I remember*.
(adverb phrase modifying the adjective *bigger*)

Adjective Clauses

A subordinate clause that modifies or describes a noun or a pronoun is called an *adjective clause* or a *relative clause*.

Examples:
The man *whom you saw* is the town police chief. (Modifies "man")
The president presented a purple heart to the man *who lost his leg in war*. (Modifies "man")
Do you know the place *where I left my scarf*?

Relative Pronouns

Back in the chapter about pronouns, we told you that there was another kind of pronoun – the relative pronoun – that we would save for later. *Relative pronouns* are pronouns used to begin subordinate clauses, especially adjective clauses. They tell, refer to, or are related to a word or idea that preceded them.

Some relative pronouns are:
who   whom   whose   which   that   what

Examples:
The man *whom* you saw is the town police chief.
The president presented a purple heart to the man *who* lost his leg in Iraq.
The house *that* I built is sturdy.
I do not know *whose* that is.

Some relative pronouns also have indefinite forms.

Some indefinite relative pronouns:
whoever   whomever   whatever   whichever

Examples:
My mother said I could invite *whomever I pleased*.
Whoever took the cookies needs to return them.
This spoiled child gets *whatever he wants*.

When you are trying to choose the appropriate relative pronoun, remember the following:

→ *Who* (and *whoever*) refers back to a person or people. *Who* is the **subject** of the relative clause. You can tell if *who* is correct if the phrase still makes sense when you substitute a subject pronoun, such as *he, she,* or *it*.

Example:
> The boy *who asked me to the dance* is in my math class. (*Who* is the subject of the verb *asked*: "*He* asked")

→ *Whom* (and *whomever*) refers back to a person or people as well, but it is the **object** of the relative clause. You can test whether whom is correct by substituting one of the object pronouns: *him, her, me, us,* or *them*.

Examples:
> The boy *whom I asked* to the dance is in my math class. (*Whom* refers back to *boy* and is the direct object of the verb *asked*; *I* is the clause's subject: "I asked *him*")
>
> My children, *for whom I sacrificed everything*, are now college graduates. (*Whom*, referring back to *children*, is the object of the preposition *for*; *I* is the clause's subject: "I sacrificed for *them*")
>
> Those girls, *one of whom is my best friend*, go to my school. (*Whom*, referring back to *girls*, is the object of the preposition *of*; *one* is the clause's subject: "One of *them* is my best friend")

→ *Whose* also refers back to a person or people. It conveys possession.

Examples:
> The girl *whose house this is* said we could throw a party.
> I know many parents *whose children attend that school*.

→ *That* refers back to a place, thing, or idea. The information *that* introduces is critical to the meaning of the sentence, because it is highly specific to that place, thing, or idea.

Examples:
> This is an opportunity *that I cannot afford to pass up*. (What kind of opportunity? One I can't afford to pass up. Knowing what kind is important to the meaning of the sentence.)
> The fact *that you lied to me* is more troublesome than what you actually said. (What specific fact? The fact that you lied to me. Knowing the details of the fact is essential to the meaning of the sentence.)

→ *Which* also refers back to a place, thing, or idea. However, the information *which* introduces generally is additional and not critical to the sentence's main meaning. Usually a *which* clause will be offset by commas.

Examples:
> Latin, *which happens to be my favorite subject*, is a dwindling academic field. (*Which* refers to *Latin*, but the fact that Latin is my favorite subject is not essential to the main meaning of the sentence – that Latin is a dwindling academic field.)
> We took a car ride through Monterey, California, *which is the setting of many John Steinbeck novels*. (*Which* refers to Monterey, but the fact that Monterey is the setting of many

Steinbeck novels is not essential to the main meaning of the sentence – that we took a car ride through Monterey.)

However, *which* is always used when it is the object of a preposition, such as *to* or *for*, that introduces the adjective clause.

Examples:

We scrutinized the surface *to which the fingerprint powder adhered*. (Here *which* refers back to *surface* and is the object of the preposition *to*.)
Spelunking was not the activity *for which he had signed up*. (*Which* refers back to *activity* and is the object of the preposition *for*.)

*Note that sometimes the relative pronoun is left out. Often in narration or conversation we say, "the book Sam read..." instead of "the book *that* Sam read...."

Exercise 2:

Fill in the blank with the appropriate relative pronoun.

1. The book _____ I read yesterday was interesting.
2. I looked up the address to _____ I will send this package.
3. I do not know the girl about _____ you are talking.
4. Technology is a subject about _____ they know very little.
5. The woodchuck _____ ate the tomatoes hid under the bush.
6. Do you know _____ I left my keys?
7. The sandwich _____ I ate was absolutely delicious.
8. This is the table on _____ I put the book.
9. I know a man _____ daughter is in medical school.
10. Danny is the boy _____ wrote me love letters.
11. Sandra is the girl for _____ he wrote poems.
12. This city, _____ is home to millions, has many excellent restaurants.

Noun Clauses

A *noun clause* may perform any function that a noun would. It may be a subject, an object, an adverbial objective, a predicate nominative, or an appositive. Noun clauses may begin with a pronoun, an interrogative adverb, a subordinating conjunction, or an expletive (ex. *that*), a word that acts as a sort of "filler" and whose only grammatical purpose is to introduce a noun clause. Like all clauses, noun clauses have a subject and a verb.

Examples:
What I did is a secret.
That is *what I told you*.
I would like to eat *whatever you would like to cook for me*.
We discussed *whether we should go see Aunt Martha*.
Everyone knows *that yellow is the best color in the rainbow*. (*that* is an expletive here; the sentence would also make sense without it)

Indirect Questions

The idea of an *indirect question* can be a little bit tricky. In essence, an indirect question is a question embedded in a sentence so that it no longer asks the question directly.

Examples:
I don't know *how many sheep there are*.
→ *How many sheep there are* is a close relative of the question *How many sheep are there?* However, this sentence states that you don't know the anwer to that question. Thus the question is a clause embedded in the larger sentence, which is a statement.

I asked him *what he was doing*.
→ *What he was doing* is a close relative of the question *What was he doing?* Here you are stating that you asked this particular question.

I wonder *if it will rain tomorrow*.
→ *If it will rain tomorrow* is a close relative of the question *Will it rain tomorrow?* However, it's not asking a question when it is placed into the sentence above. Rather, the sentence states that you are wondering about this question.

Exercise 3:

Underline the noun clauses and identify what function they are serving (subject, direct object, etc.).

1. You'll never guess what I did today.

2. What I did bothered my family.

3. That he didn't know how to cook was quite obvious.

4. I love tasting whatever other people think is good.

5. From what you are telling me, I cannot make an accurate diagnosis.

6. I know that purple is the color of royalty.

7. He told me what he knew.

8. Martha knew what he said was true.

9. His problem is that he is a procrastinator.

10. Joy loves that her dog is small.

11. Allie reads whatever books she can find.

12. Some people say that aliens exist on Mars.

13. Your issue was that you were not assertive enough with your boss.

14. What you are looking at right now is a very famous painting.

15. A good secretary sees what needs to be done and does it.

16. I don't know whether it will snow tomorrow.

Review: Clauses

Exercise 4:

Underline the subordinate clause in each of the following sentences and determine whether it is an adverb, adjective, or noun clause.

1. You will find the answer that you are looking for in this book.

2. Until the criminal spends twenty years in jail, he will not be allowed to leave.

3. The pond where the frogs live is also inhabited by grasshoppers.

4. Show me that you are not a coward.

5. I would like to eat whatever you would like to serve me.

6. While I was walking to the store, I bumped into my neighbor.

7. What is it that you need?

8. The boy turned on the stove, even though his mother warned him not to.

9. Number 5 is the problem that you answered incorrectly.

10. Carlos always appreciates what his family gives him.

11. Provided that you eat healthily and work out, you will stay in good shape.

12. Reading novels, which is a good way to expand your vocabulary, can be fun as well.

13. That she was unprepared was evident.

14. My grandmother believes that no one ever actually landed on the moon.

15. I left my house after the rain subsided.

16. I don't know the man about whom you are talking.

17. Believe in what you think is right.

18. Is your sister the person whom Jeremy is taking to the dance?

19. As soon as Mike finishes playing his game, we will go out to dinner.

20. The police officer claimed that the driver of the red car was at fault.

21. Sometimes James's father acts as if he is a dictator.

22. Sara told me the address to which I should send the letter.

23. I know that Jim hates spaghetti.

24. Unless Dan first admits he has a problem, he will not be able to fix it.

25. I need to find the girl whose wallet I have.

26. Greg found what you were looking for.

27. Answer the phone that is ringing!

28. Before you leave for lunch, make sure you have some money.

29. Ryan told Susan where the cookies from the jar went.

30. The baby cries whenever she needs something.

Diagramming

To diagram *adverb clauses*, the subordinate clause receives its own sentence line below the main sentence line. The subordinating conjunction is placed on a dotted line connecting the two. If the adverb clause modifies the main verb, the dotted line is between the verb of the independent clause and the verb in the subordinate clause. If the adverb clause modifies an adjective or adverb, the dotted line connects the adverb or adjective to the verb of the subordinate clause.

Example:

If you study, you will pass.

      you   will pass
                If

      you   study

The adverb clause *if you study* is introduced by the subordinating conjunction *if*. This adverb clause modifies the verb phrase *will pass*, since it describes the circumstances under which *will pass* takes place. Therefore, we connect *will pass*, the main verb, and *study*, the verb in the subordinate clause, with a dotted line. *If*, the subordinating conjunction that links the two clauses, is placed on that dotted line.

Like adverb clauses, *adjective clauses* are diagrammed on their own sentence line below the main sentence line and are connected by a dotted line running from the relative pronoun to the word it modifies.

Examples:

The snake that ate the squirrel left.

```
        snake        left
         The
                that    ate    squirrel
                                  the
```

The relative pronoun *that* is the subject of its relative clause; its antecedent is *snake*.

The man for whom you are looking is sick

```
        man      is    sick
         The
        you   are looking
                     for
                         whom
```

The relative pronoun *whom* is the object of a preposition in its relative clause; its antecedent is *man*.

Noun clauses are diagrammed the same way as infinitive clauses, leaving out the *to*. The noun clause is placed in the position where it grammatically belongs. If a noun clause is introduced by an expletive (usually *that, if,* or *whether*), the expletive is diagrammed above the noun clause and is connected to the noun clause's verb with a dotted line.

Examples:

What I did is a secret.

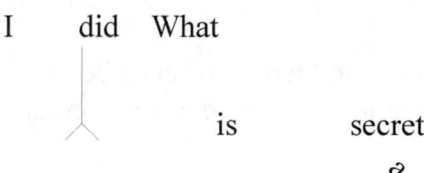

The noun clause is introduced by the interrogative pronoun *what*. *What* is the direct object of the noun clause (*I* is the subject). The noun clause is the subject of the sentence.

That is what I told you.

```
                I    told    what
That    is                   you
```

This noun clause is also introduced by the interrogative pronoun *what*. *What* is the direct object of the noun clause (*I* is the subject). The noun clause is the direct object of the sentence.

I wonder if she will like the gift.

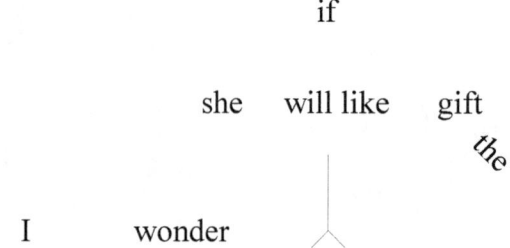

The noun clause is the direct object of the sentence. *If* is an expletive, as it serves no real purpose other than to introduce the noun clause.

Diagramming Exercises

Diagram the following sentences.

1. Fran failed the test because she had not studied.

2. Although they elected him president, they did not consider him a good man.

3. Unless jogging makes you too tired, you should try it someday for exercise.

4. If I give you some money, will you run to the store for a few groceries that I need?

5. Your sister will come to your recital, even if she must miss her favorite show on TV.

6. Because my brother's current roommate seems friendly and converses well, we invited him to dinner.

7. The dancing bear that you saw in the zoo just had a baby!

8. Evan gave Priscilla, who was his first girlfriend, a beautiful bouquet of blooming roses.

9. Is that the girl whose parents you met last week at graduation?

10 Can you direct this message to the mailbox of the person to whom it is addressed?

11. That's the thing I was going to tell you about.

12. I won the race because I was the one who swam fastest.

13. I know that you are a diligent and hardworking student.

14. My biggest problem is that I do not have time for skiing or swimming, my favorite activities.

15. It is unlikely that many people will come to the performance late.

16. Yesterday we asked them whether we should give a dollar to the laughing musician who played guitar nearby.

Glossary of Grammatical Terms

Noun – a person, place, thing, or idea. **Proper nouns** name one particular person, place, thing, or idea (*Arthur Miller, Vietnam, the Parthenon, Buddhism, Ayer Rock*). **Common nouns** name a thing or idea in its more general form (*playwright, country, building, religion, rock*), and can be singular or plural. **Collective nouns** treat a group of things as a single entity (*herd, flock, pair*) and usually take a singular verb. A **noun of direct address** is exactly what it sounds like: a noun used to address someone directly (Would you please pass the potatoes, *Colin*?)

Verb – an action or state of being (*to run* is an **action verb**; *to be, to feel,* and *to appear* are some **state of being verbs**, also known as **linking verbs**).

Subject – the noun or pronoun that is doing the action of the verb (the "who," or actor in the sentence: *Jose* runs cross-country), or that is in a particular state of being (*She* feels lousy.)

Adjective – a word that modifies, or describes, a noun (the *pretty* girl, *one* cup)

Article – the words *a, an,* and *the*. A subclass of adjectives indicating whether you are speaking of a specific thing, or a class of things in general (*a* tornado, *the* storm).

Demonstrative Adjective – the words *this, that, these,* and *those*, when used to modify a noun (I hate *that* class; I love *these* books).

Adverb – a word that modifies, or describes, a verb, another adverb, or an adjective (run *quickly; very* hastily; *quite* attractive)

Adverbial Objective – a noun or group of words that acts like an adverb by answering questions such as *How? Where? When?* or *To what extent?* (When are you visiting Washington? We're visiting Washington *this spring*.)

Predicate Nominative – a noun or noun phrase that follows a linking verb and renames or gives more information about the subject (Leila is *a blonde;* Sam became *a doctor specializing in neuralgia*).

Predicate Adjective – an adjective or adjective phrase that follows a linking verb and gives more information about the subject (Sarah's hair is *blonde*; John is *known for his sense of humor*).

Subject Complement – this term includes both **predicate nominatives** and **predicate adjectives**, because both work with linking verbs to "complement" the subject by giving more descriptive information about it.

Object Complement – a word that completes an action verb. (Tamara is running *the show* answers the question: What is she running? Andy was named *commander* of the vessel answers the question: What was he named?)

Preposition – a word used to connect nouns and phrases and show their relationship (*about, above, below, over, under, of, to, for, from, beside, next to;* They waited *under* the awning *during* the brief rainstorm).

Prepositional Phrase – a phrase beginning with a preposition and including a noun, often with modifiers (the apartment *on the top floor*; the book *about carnivorous dinosaurs*; a gift *for Kevin*).

Adjective Phrase – a prepositional phrase that modifies a noun. (The book *of Aesop's fables* was open to the story, "The Grasshopper and the Ants." Which book? The book *of Aesop's fables*. The door *to the house* was locked. Which door? The door *to the house*)

Adverb Phrase – a prepositional phrase that modifies a verb. (He placed it *on the table*. Where was it placed? *On the table*. She handled the dynamite *with extreme caution*. How did she handle it? *With extreme caution*.)

Object of the Preposition – the noun in a prepositional phrase. (On the *table*, over the *moon*, around the *world*, with dark *hair*)

Personal Pronoun – a word that substitutes for a particular noun as either subject or object (*I, you, he,*

she, it, we, and *they* are **personal subjective pronouns**; *me, you, him, her, us,* and *them* are **personal objective pronouns**). Personal pronouns may also be possessive, reflexive, or intensive (see below).
Possessive Pronoun – a type of personal pronoun that comes in two forms, it can either modify a noun (*my* car, *your* book, *his* donkey, *her* iPod, *its* chirrup, *our* religion, *their* cattle) or stand alone as a substitute for a possessive noun (*mine, yours, his, hers, its, ours, theirs:* Which car is Mary's? The green one is *hers*).
Reflexive Pronoun – these words (*myself, yourself, himself, itself, herself, oneself, ourselves, yourselves, themselves*) are used to indicate an action one does to oneself (She brushed *herself* off after jumping in the leaf pile).
Intensive Pronoun – comprising the same group of words as reflexive pronouns, they are used instead to emphasize the subject of the sentence (I *myself* saw President Obama sneaking a cigarette offstage).
Interrogative Pronoun – a pronoun used to ask a question (*who, whom, whose, which, what*: Which movie did you see?).
Relative Pronoun – a pronoun that introduces a subordinate clause and refers to, or is related to, a word or idea that preceded it (the man *who* protested outside the embassy; *who* refers back to *man*)
Demonstrative Pronoun – similar to the demonstrative adjective, but it stands alone in place of a noun, instead of acting as a modifier before a noun (*this, that, these, those*: "*These* are Helen's, and *those* are Lupe's" [pronouns] vs. "*These* shoes belong to Helen" [adjective]).
Indefinite Pronoun – a word that refers generally or imprecisely to a person or people, places, things, or ideas (*all, anybody, both, everything, either, few, no one, somebody, whichever, whomever, one, much*: "Store closing sale: *Everything* must go!"). Some of these same words may function as adjectives because they modify a noun, instead of standing in for it ("A *few* decided not to participate" [pronoun] vs. "A *few* kids must stay to clean up afterward" [adjective]).
Pronoun Antecedent – the noun to which a pronoun refers ("*Tammy's* purse is on the desk. Please get her purse."
Verb Phrase – a main verb plus its helping verbs (He *might have been* badly injured! I *can ride* a unicycle). Some helping verbs have an infinitive form; others (*will, shall, should, would, ought, may, might, must, can,* and *could*) do not.
Verb Tense – the time at which the action of the verb was, is, or will be completed. The most basic tenses are the simple past, present, and future.
Voice – a verb is in the **active voice** if the subject of the sentence is performing the verb (Mrs. Dowling *read* the book aloud to her class); the **passive voice** occurs when the subject is having something done to it (The book *was read* aloud by Mrs. Dowling.) Generally, the active voice is preferable.
Mood – verbs have three moods: indicative, subjunctive, or imperative. The **imperative mood** is used in a command (*Do* your homework!) and implies the subject *you*, either singular or plural. The **indicative mood** is the most common, used in discussing something that the speaker regards as undisputed fact or truth (Karen *did* her homework). The **subjunctive mood** indicates doubt, uncertainty, wishing, or dependence on some other condition. It may need helping verbs such as *might, may, should,* or *would* (I hoped that he *would help* me with my homework).
Conjunction – a word or words that join two sentence elements. There are several types: **coordinating conjunctions** (*for, and, not, but, or, yet,* and *so*); **correlative conjunctions** (*either/or, both/and, whether/or, neither/nor,* and *not only/but also*); and subordinating conjunctions (*after, although, as much as, if, unless,* and *until* are some examples).
Compound Subject – two or more nouns joined by a conjunction (Mary-Kate *and* Ashley Olsen; *not only* cats, *but* dogs). Two or more nouns joined by a conjuction can also form a **compound direct object**, depending on how they occur in the sentence. **Compound predicate adjectives** (short *but* handsome) and **compound prepositional phrases** (over the river *and* through the woods) are also

connected by conjunctions. A **compound sentence** consists of two independent clauses linked by a conjunction.

Interjection – A word used by itself to express strong emotion (Oh! Hooray! What? Darn!).

Appositive – a noun or noun phrase that renames and gives more information about the noun that precedes it (The president of the United States, *Barack Obama*)

Verbals – These are verb forms that act as another part of speech. The **gerund** acts as a noun and is formed by adding *-ing* to the root (*Swimming* is my favorite exercise). The **participle** acts as an adjective: The present participle is formed by adding *-ing* (the *fascinating* girl), while the past participle is formed by adding *-ed* (the *reinforced* bridge).

Infinitive – the basic, or pure, form of a verb, it is usually preceded by *to* (*to march, to paint, to study*). It is also a verbal that, along with any related words, can act as a noun (He loved *to dance*); an adjective (their desire *to see all Paris*); or an adverb (I decided he was too grouchy *to approach*). An **infinitive clause** will have its own subject, which is also the object of the main verb (She asked *me to write down the test questions*.)

Phrase – a group of connected words that does not contain a subject and a verb. These include **prepositional phrases** (*over my head*); **appositive phrases** (Katharine, *the editor of this workbook*); **gerund phrases** (*Running cross-country* is my fall sport); **participial phrases** (The cat, *spying the dog*, ran away; the pipe, *blocked by ice*, sprang a leak); and **infinitive phrases** (*To hunt in November* is an invigorating pastime).

Clause – a group of connected words that contains a subject and a verb. An **independent clause** can stand alone as a sentence (The cat jumped up on the shelf). A **subordinate clause**, also known as a **dependent clause**, is connected to the main independent clause with a subordinating conjunction (He asked Sarah to go *after he found out I was unavailable*). An **adverb clause** modifies a verb, an adjective, or another adverb (Lisa goes *wherever her husband goes*). An **adjective clause**, also known as a **relative clause**, modifies a noun or pronoun (The people *who came to my door* were Jehovah's Witnesses); they often begin with a relative pronoun. A **noun clause** acts as a subject or object (I was told *that she likes anchovies on her pizza*).

Expletive – a type of interjection (*Good heavens!*); also, "filler" words that act as dummy subjects (*It* is raining; *There* are hundreds of people) or that introduce a noun clause (Everyone knows *that* blondes have more fun), but are not necessary to the meaning of the sentence.

ANSWER KEY

CHAPTER ONE: NOUNS AND ACTION VERBS

Exercise 1:

1. concrete 2. abstract 3. both 4. concrete 5. concrete 6. abstract 7. concrete 8. abstract 9. concrete 10. concrete

Exercise 2:

1. common 2. proper 3. common 4. common 5. proper 6. common 7. proper 8. proper 9. common 10. proper

Exercise 3:

1. singular 2. singular 3. plural 4. singular 5. singular 6. plural 7. plural 8. singular 9. singular 10. plural

Exercise 4:

1. collective 2. not collective 3. collective 4. collective 5. not collective 6. not collective

Exercise 5:

"It is simply this. That <u>Space</u>, as our <u>mathematicians</u> have it, is spoken of as having three <u>dimensions</u>, which one may call <u>Length</u>, <u>Breadth</u>, and <u>Thickness</u>, and is always definable by <u>reference</u> to three <u>planes</u>, each at right <u>angles</u> to the others. But some philosophical <u>people</u> have been asking why three <u>dimensions</u> particularly—why not another <u>direction</u> at right <u>angles</u> to the other three – and have even tried to construct a Four-Dimension <u>geometry</u>. <u>Professor Simon Newcomb</u> was expounding this to the <u>New York Mathematical Society</u> only a <u>month</u> or so ago. You know how on a flat <u>surface</u>, which has only two <u>dimensions</u>, we can represent a <u>figure</u> of a three-dimensional <u>solid</u>, and similarly they think that by <u>models</u> of three <u>dimensions</u> they could represent <u>one of four</u>—if they could master the <u>perspective</u> of the <u>thing</u>. See?"

Exercise 6:

"We write these <u>words</u> now, many <u>miles</u> distant from the <u>spot</u> at which, <u>year</u> after <u>year</u>, we met on that <u>day</u>, a merry and joyous <u>circle</u>. Many of the <u>hearts</u> that throbbed so gaily then, have ceased to beat; many of the <u>looks</u> that shone so brightly then, have ceased to glow; the <u>hands</u> we grasped, have grown cold; the <u>eyes</u> we sought, have hid their <u>lustre</u> in the <u>grave</u>; and yet the old <u>house</u>, the <u>room</u>, the merry <u>voices</u> and smiling <u>faces</u>, the <u>jest</u>, the <u>laugh</u>, the most minute and trivial <u>circumstances</u> connected with those happy <u>meetings</u>, crowd upon our <u>mind</u> at each <u>recurrence</u> of the <u>season</u>, as if the last <u>assemblage</u> had been but yesterday! Happy, happy <u>Christmas</u>, that can win us back to the <u>delusions</u> of our childish <u>days</u>; that can recall to the old <u>man</u> the <u>pleasures</u> of his <u>youth</u>; that can transport the <u>sailor</u> and the <u>traveler</u>, <u>thousands</u> of <u>miles</u> away, back to his own <u>fireside</u> and his quiet <u>home</u>!"

Note: The word thousands *in the last sentence is a noun acting as an adjective modifying* miles. *An*

argument could be made to exclude it from the list of nouns in the passage for this reason.

Exercise 7:

1. concrete, common, singular, and collective **2.** concrete, proper, plural, and not collective **3.** abstract, common, singular, and not collective **4.** abstract, proper, singular and not collective **5.** concrete, common, singular, and not collective

Exercise 8:

1. Sarah <u>cooks</u> a lot of pizza in her free time. (present)
2. It <u>rained</u> cats and dogs last night. (neither)
3. That pig <u>is giving</u> birth to piglets! (present progressive)
4. My mother <u>uses</u> the treadmill every morning. (present)
5. When Julia <u>drinks</u> water instead of soda, she <u>loses</u> weight. (present, present)
6. Because Melissa <u>worked</u> very hard in high school, she <u>attends</u> an excellent college. (neither, present)
7. That boy <u>made</u> a lot of money when he <u>mowed</u> his neighbor's lawn last summer. (neither, neither)
8. Mr. Jones really <u>wants</u> a raise, so he <u>is working</u> extra hours at the office. (present, present progressive)
9. Liz <u>was studying</u> physics when the phone <u>rang</u>. (neither, neither)
10. Colleges <u>look</u> for students who <u>participate</u> in a wide range of activities. (present, present)

Exercise 9:

Note that the following are example sentences. Your sentences will vary.

1. I read a lot of books. (present) Sam is reading a long novel. (present progressive)
2. Woods surround the cabin. (present) The angry protesters are surrounding the town hall. (present progressive)
3. My little brother annoys me. (present) Her dog is annoying my cat. (present progressive)
4. I buy seeds for my garden each year. (present) Jane is buying a book from the Andover Bookstore. (present progressive)
5. Habitat for Humanity builds many houses in the United States each year. (present) Susan's father is building a dollhouse for her. (present progressive)

Exercise 10:

1. eats **2.** brushes **3.** is knocking **4.** takes **5.** watches **6.** is starting **7.** are taking **8.** eats **9.** is surfing

Exercise 11:

Note that the following are example sentences. Your sentences will vary.

1. Cheese goes well with crackers.
2. Jack plays soccer for an elite team.
3. Dictionaries help students understand new words.
4. Dogs bark at unfamiliar people.
5. Christians celebrate Christmas in different ways around the world.

Exercise 12:

1. paperboy **2.** cookies **3.** Sasha **4.** train

Exercise 13:

1. The <u>chef</u> is preparing a (salad).

2. The <u>diner</u> leaves a (tip).

3. The <u>author</u> is writing a (novel).

4. College <u>students</u> drink a lot of (coffee).

5. The <u>boy</u> dropped the (basketball).

6. <u>Sean</u> plays (basketball) very well.

7. My <u>teacher</u> tells (stories) in class.

8. The <u>Gap</u> sells good-quality (jeans) to people of all ages.

9. The <u>man</u> ate the (cow).

10. The <u>shark</u> ate the (man).

Exercise 14:

Note that the following are example sentences. Your sentences will vary.

1. Jared plays baseball with his friends.
2. The clown is blowing up a balloon for the child.
3. The baby saw the mug on the counter and reached for it.
4. Ellen writes music, and also enjoys listening to it.
5. Mary bought curtains for her new house.
6. The customer put the bag into her car.
7. The man fought the lion.
8. The lion ate the man.

Exercise 15:

1. Peter gives his (wife) a <u>bouquet</u>.

2. Jean is bringing (Michael) <u>dinner</u>.

3. The gymnast wins a <u>trophy.</u>

4. Jamie is drinking <u>soda.</u>

5. Tom hugs <u>Judy.</u>

6. Tom gives a <u>hug</u> to Judy.

7. The cat is chasing the <u>squirrel</u>!

8. Joe pays <u>money</u> to the cashier.

9. Joe pays the (cashier).
10. Isabelle tells her (mother) lies.
11. Ms. Foster shows her (student) the answer.
12. The boy is going to the mall.
13. The grocer gives the receipt to the customer.
14. Jake offers his (girlfriend) a ride home.
15. Peter reads (Eugene) a book.
16. Peter reads to Eugene.
17. The secretary brings my (clients) coffee.

Exercise 16:

Note that the following are example sentences. Your sentences will vary.

1. I gave Josh the book.
2. Jake bought flowers for his mother.
3. Macy bought Ian a sweater.
4. I love New York, the city where I live.
5. Mrs. Underwood gave John an eraser.
6. The salesman sold the family a car.
7. George drove a race car.
8. The dog chewed the curtains to tatters.
9. The boss paid Rachel a higher salary than Michael.
10. The servants brought the queen dinner.
11. The cashier despises William.
12. The paramedics gave the runner water.

Exercise 17:

Note that the following are example sentences. Your sentences will vary.

1. Joe likes Lila. He gave Lila flowers.
2. Tom saw the man watching him. He gave the man a nasty look.
3. John met his new doctor. He gave his doctor his health records.
4. The professor met his student for lunch. He gave the student an F on her paper.
5. Her parents sent Penelope to boarding school. Her teachers all gave Penelope good grades.
6. I found a child on my doorstep. His family did not give the child a good home.
7. I greeted my teacher. I handed my teacher the essay I wrote.
8. I finally met my long-lost mother. I gave my mother a photo album.

Exercise 18:

1. Transitive - Johnathan is kicking the ball.
2. Transitive - The monster is eating Shane for breakfast.

3. Intransitive
4. Transitive - Now, he has a <u>stomachache</u>.
5. Transitive - The boy bought <u>books</u> from the store.
6. Intransitive
7. Intransitive
8. Transitive - Yolanda really loves <u>Monopoly</u>.

Diagrammed Exercises:

1. Flowers bloom.

```
    Flowers  |  bloom
```

Flowers is the subject of the sentence, and *bloom* is its present tense action verb.

2. People breathe air.

```
    People  |  breathe  |  air
```

People is the subject of the sentence, *breathe* is the action verb, and *air* is the direct object, the recipient of the action *breathe*. (What do people breathe? Air.)

3. Do dogs swim?

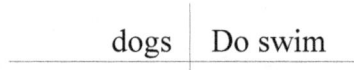

Dogs is the subject of the sentence, and *do swim* is the verb. *Do swim* is an example of the present emphatic, a tense often used in questions. *Do* is capitalized in the diagram because it is the first word of the sentence.

4. Girls are eating pie.

```
    Girls  |  are eating  |  pie
```

Girls is the subject of the sentence, and *are eating* is the present progressive action verb. *Pie* is the direct object. (What are the girls eating? Pie.)

5. Jane gives Sarah gifts.

```
_____Jane_____|___gives___|___gifts___
              |     \
              |      \Sarah
```

    Jane is the subject of the sentence, and *gives* is the present tense action verb. *Gifts* is the direct object, and *Sarah* is the indirect object. (What is Jane giving? Gifts. To whom? To Sarah.)

6. Ben is running.

```
_____Ben_____|___is running___
```

    Ben is the subject of the sentence, and *is running* is the present progressive action verb. Here, we see the verb run in its *intranstive* form; it has no direct object.

7. Ben is running races.

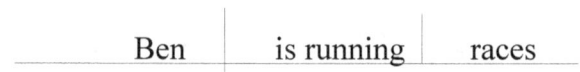

    As in the sentence above, *Ben* is the subject of the sentence, and *is running* is the present progressive action verb. However, in this sentence, we see the verb in its *transitive* form, taking the direct object *races*. (What is Ben running? Races.)

8. Veronica kicks basketballs.

```
_____Veronica_____|___dribbles___|___basketballs___
```

    Veronica is the subject of the sentence, *dribbles* is the present tense action verb, and *basketballs* is the direct object. (What does Veronica dribble? Basketballs.)

9. Whales eat plankton.

```
_____Whales_____|___eat___|___
      plankton  |
```

    Whales is the subject of the sentence, *eat* is the present tense action verb, and *plankton* is the direct object. (What do whales eat? Plankton.)

10. Children give Mrs. Benson headaches.

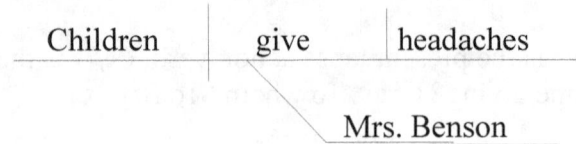

Children is the subject of the sentence, and *give* is the present tense action verb. *Headaches* is the direct object, and *Mrs. Benson* is the indirect object. (What do children give? Headaches. To whom? To Mrs. Benson.)

11. Amanda bakes children cookies.

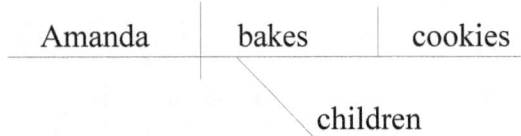

Amanda is the subject of the sentence, and *bakes* is the present tense action verb. *Cookies* is the direct object, and *children* is the indirect object. (What does Amanda bake? Cookies. For whom? For children.)

12. Doreen is buying Jake dinner.

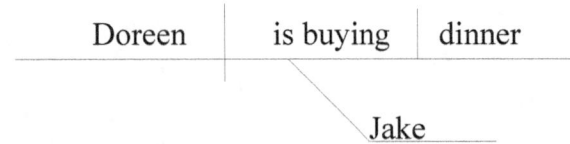

Doreen is the subject of the sentence, and *is buying* is the present progressive action verb. *Dinner* is the direct object, and *Jake* is the indirect object. (What is Doreen buying? Dinner. For whom? For Jake.)

*Notice that in these last two sentences especially, diagramming can help us distinguish the meaning of a sentence and vice versa. In example 11, for instance, the diagonal line connecting *children* to *bakes* shows us that *children* is the indirect object. If, however, *children* had been misplaced and was put where *cookies* is, we would have an entirely different sentence. Amanda would be baking children, instead of baking cookies *for* them. The same applies to example 12. If *Jake* were the direct object,

Doreen would be buying Jake, instead of buying dinner *for* him.

In this way, diagramming can help us distinguish between the parts of a sentence so that we can better understand their meaning as a whole.

CHAPTER TWO: ADJECTIVES, ADVERBS, AND STATE OF BEING VERBS

Exercise 1:

"The moon shone <u>bright</u>; a sprinkling of snow covered the ground, and I reflected that she might, possibly, have taken it into her head to walk about the garden, for refreshment. I did detect a figure creeping along the <u>inner</u> fence of the park; but it was not my <u>young</u> mistress: on its emerging into the light, I recognized one of the grooms. He stood a <u>considerable</u> period, viewing the carriage-road through the grounds; then started off at a <u>brisk</u> pace, as if he had detected something, and reappeared presently, leading Miss's pony; and there she was, just <u>dismounted</u>, and walking by its side. The man took his charge stealthily across the grass towards the stable. Cathy entered by the <u>casement</u> window of the <u>drawing</u> room, and glided noiselessly up to where I awaited her. She put the door gently to, slipped off her <u>snowy</u> shoes, untied her hat, and was proceeding, <u>unconscious</u> of my espionage, to lay aside her mantle, when I suddenly rose and revealed myself. The surprise petrified her an instant: she uttered an <u>inarticulate</u> exclamation, and stood <u>fixed</u>."

Note: The adjectives casement *in "casement window" and* drawing *in "drawing room" are adjectives that are paired so frequently with these nouns that they form a sort of compound noun. These words still are adjectives, however, and should be classified as such. By contrast,* carriage *in "carriage-road" is part of a compound noun, as indicated by the hyphen. Note also that* bright *and* fixed *might appear to be modifying the verbs* shone *and* stood*; however,* shone *and* stood *appear to be operating here as linking verbs, i.e.* moon=bright *and* she=fixed. *also, the adverb forms of* bright *and* fixed *are* brightly *and* fixedly.

Exercise 2:

Note that the following are example sentences. Your sentences will vary.

1. Dark walls make a room appear smaller.
2. Rare steak can contain bacteria that make you sick.
3. The bright sun coming through the windows is blinding my vision.
4. Hot soups are great for cold winter days.
5. The height of the cliff was dizzying.
6. The joyful girl skipped through the meadow.
7. The sight of the mountain ranges in Alaska is breathtaking.
8. The youthful man continued to play tennis well into his retirement.
9. The enormous dog towered above other dogs of its breed.
10. He needs to wash his smelly socks.

Exercise 3:

1. Adam walked <u>stealthily</u> across the capture-the-flag field. (verb)
2. Hilary waved <u>very</u> <u>shyly.</u> at Josh as he called her name. (adverb; verb)
3. Josephine, who was <u>very</u> upset with Nathan, kicked him. (adjective)
4. Thomas made his parents dinner <u>yesterday</u>. (verb)
5. Brian loves Rita <u>intensely</u>. (verb)
6. Peter is an <u>exceedingly</u> attractive man. (adjective)
7. Bridget is <u>not</u> studying math. (verb)

8. Abby acted <u>quite</u> <u>well</u> in her school play. (adverb; verb)
9. Amy <u>always</u> wears flip flops. (verb)
10. <u>Clearly</u> upset, Nina ran home crying. (adjective)
11. Jill is taking the SATs <u>tomorrow</u>. (verb)

Exercise 4:

Note that the following are example sentences. Your sentences will vary.

1. The little girl patted the dog gently. (verb)
2. That cat is quite vicious. (adjective)
3. She ran extremely well in the 100 meter race. (adverb)
4. He always reads the headline news. (verb)
5. You should never say never. (verb)
6. Henry did well on his exam. (verb)
7. The apparently happy couple suddenly got a divorce. (adjective)
8. I often see dead grass here. (verb)
9. She sang the lullaby softly. (verb)
10. She rarely eats ice cream. (verb)

Exercise 5:

1. Come <u>here</u>! (adverb)
2. Come <u>this way</u>! (adverbial objective)
3. <u>Tomorrow</u> Lauren is going to the store. (adverb)
4. Vicky is moving to New York <u>next Wednesday</u>. (adverbial objective)
5. Tammy deposited the paycheck <u>the next day</u>. (adverbial objective)
6. Jason <u>never</u> says hello. (adverb)
7. Penny lives <u>next door</u>. (adverbial objective)
8. Kelly is <u>extremely</u> beautiful. (adverb)
9. Kelly is <u>24 years</u> old. (adverbial objective)
10. <u>Sometimes</u> Ned drives <u>a different way</u>. (adverb; adverbial objective)
11. Wilma and George <u>often</u> talk <u>all night</u>. (adverb; adverbial objective)
12. The pool is <u>nearly</u> <u>ten feet</u> deep. (adverb; adverbial objective)

Exercise 6:

1. linking **2.** action **3.** action **4.** linking **5.** linking **6.** linking **7.** action **8.** action **9. linking** **10.** action
11. linking **12.** linking

Exercise 7:

Note that the following are example sentences. Your sentences will vary.

1. John suddenly appeared in front of me. John appears ill.
2. I looked at the mountains. They look amazing under a full moon.
3. Mammoth sunflowers grow very tall. He is growing strong.
4. He proved the scientific theory. Dislodging the boulder proved impossible.
5. The stone remained there for the next few years. She remained young.

6. The siren sounded and the firefighters rushed out. The singer sounded nasal.
7. The truck turned the corner. The road turns uphill.

Exercise 8:

Note that the following are example sentences. Your sentences will vary.

1. The mouse is very tiny. (PA)
2. He seems obnoxious at first. (PA)
3. That animal is a kangaroo! (PN)
4. Today's snack is cheese with crackers. (PN)
5. That tourist appears to be an American. (PN)
6. Aza becomes beautiful in the novel *Fairest*, by Gail Carson Levine. (PA)
7. Ernie smells foul. (PA)

Exercise 9:

1. Bob appeared very <u>unkempt</u>. (S)
2. Ryan painted his old car <u>orange</u>. (O)
3. The small rabbit was <u>white</u>. (S)
4. Purple is my favorite <u>color</u>.(S)
5. The junior class elected the foreign exchange student <u>president</u>. (O)
6. Health is a major <u>concern</u>. (S)
7. The fast girl was the first-place <u>winner.</u> (S)
8. I consider him <u>hardworking and talented</u>. (O)
9. She is a pretty <u>girl</u>. (S)
10. Steven called him a <u>liar</u>, grabbed the CD, and ran. (O)

Diagramming Exercises:

1. Ron is a doctor.

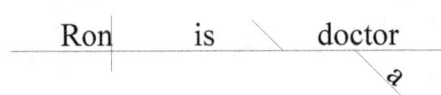

Ron is the subject of the sentence, and *is* is the linking verb. *Doctor* is the predicate nominative; it is a noun that describes and renames Ron. *A* is the article modifying *doctor*.

2. Ron is a good doctor.

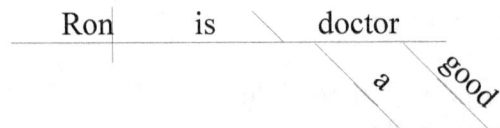

This sentence is identical to the one above it except that we have an extra adjective, *good*, modifying *doctor*, the predicate nominative.

3. Jane is very beautiful.

Jane is the subject of the sentence, *is* is the linking verb, and *beautiful* is the predicate adjective. *Very* is an intensifying adverb modifying the adjective *beautiful*, so we place it on a diagonal line connected to *beautiful*.

4. Is Jane very beautiful?

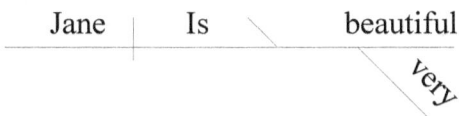

This sentence is identical to the one above it except that it's a question. It is diagrammed exactly the same way, except that we now capitalize *is* because it is the first word of the sentence.

5. The old computer is working very slowly.

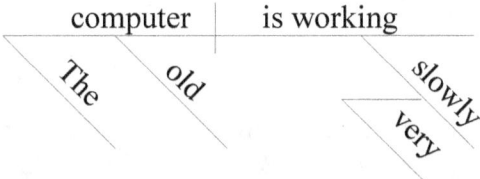

Computer is the subject of the sentence, modified by the article *the* and the adjective *old*. *Is working* is the present progressive action verb. (Now that you know linking verbs, do not assume that just because the word *is* is here, it is the main verb!) *Slowly* is an adverb modifying *is working*, and *very* is an intensifying adverb modifying *slowly*.

6. The very old computer is working slowly.

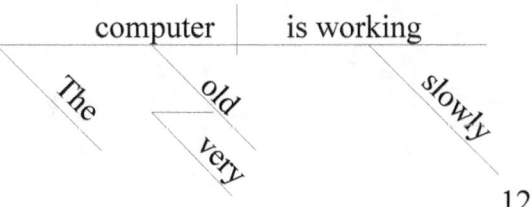

This sentence has the same seven words as the sentence above, but it has a slightly different meaning. The difference is in the placement of *very*. Whereas in the sentence above, *very* modified the adverb *slowly*, here it modifies the adjective *old*. A different word is intensified, slightly altering our understanding of the sentence.

7. These dirty children smell pizza.

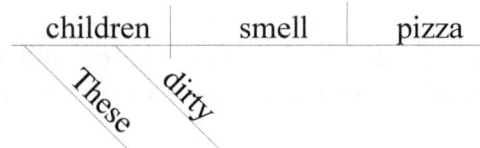

The subject of the sentence is *children,* modified by the adjectives *these* and *dirty.* The verb is *smell.* This sentence, you may notice, is similar to some of the example diagrams. Those examples used the verb *smell* first as a linking verb and then as an intransitive action verb. Here it is being used as a transitive action verb, since it takes the direct object *pizza.*

8. The very loud babies are quietly eating extremely mushy peas.

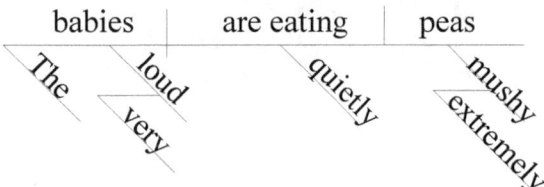

The key in this sentence is understanding which word each adverb modifies. The subject of the sentence is *babies*, and the present progressive action verb is *are eating. Peas* is the direct object of the transitive action verb. Now on to the adjectives: *The* and *loud* modify *babies*, and *mushy* modifies *peas*. Then, the adverbs: *very* intensifies the adjective *loud* (the babies aren't just loud; they are *very* loud), *quietly* modifies the verb *are eating* (telling us *how* or *in what manner* the babies are eating), and *extremely* intensifies the adjective *mushy* (those peas aren't just mushy; they are *extremely* mushy).

9. The new puppies are often extremely energetic.

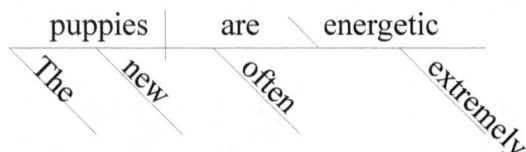

Puppies is the subject of the sentence, modified by *the* and *new*. *Are* is the linking verb, and *energetic* is the predicate adjective (puppies = energetic). The adverb *often* modifies *are*, telling us *how frequently* or *when* this happens. The intensifying adverb *extremely* modifies the adjective *energetic*, telling us *to what extent* the puppies are energetic.

10. Daniel is quite an excellent student.

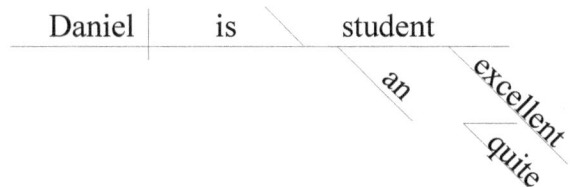

Daniel is the subject of the sentence, and *is* is the linking verb. *Student* is the predicate nominative. The article *an* modifies *student*, as does the adjective *excellent*. The adverb *quite* modifies *excellent*; not only is Daniel an excellent student, he is *quite* an excellent student.

11. The young American girls are quickly eating a small supper.

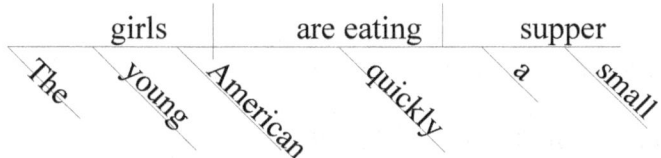

There are many modifiers in this sentence! The subject of the sentence is *girls*, the present progressive verb is *are eating*, and the direct object is *supper*. The article *the* and the adjectives *young* and *American* all modify *girls*. *American* is an example of a proper adjective, meaning that it is derived from a proper noun (in this case, *America*). *Quickly* is an adverb modifying *are eating*; it describes *how* or *in what manner* the verb is being carried out. The article *a* and the adjective *small* both modify *supper*.

12. Sam is coming this way.

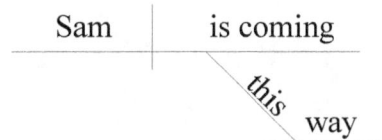

Sam is this sentence's subject, and *is coming* is a present progressive action verb. *This way* is an

129

adverbial objective; it serves the same purpose as an adverb (it answers: *Where* is he coming?), but it is a noun (*way*) modified by an adjective (*this*).

13. Patricia is making Rhonda crazy.

    Patricia | is making / crazy \ Rhonda

    Patricia is the subject of the sentence, and *is making* is the present progressive verb. *Rhonda* is the direct object, and *crazy* is an adjective being used as an object complement; *crazy* connects the verb, *is making*, to the direct object, *Rhonda*.

14. The pretty girl is giving the exceedingly handsome boy a kiss.

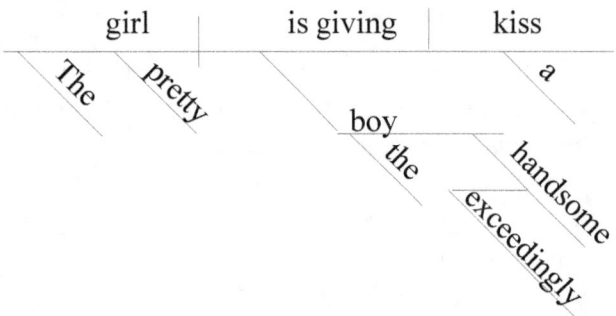

    Girl is the subject of the sentence, and *is giving* is the present progressive verb. *Kiss* is the direct obect of the transitive verb, and *boy* is the indirect object. (What does she give? A kiss. To whom? To the boy.) *The* and *pretty* modify *girl*, *a* modifies *kiss*, and *the* and *handsome* both modify *boy*. *Exceedingly* is an adverb intensifying the adjective *handsome*. The boy is not merely handsome; he is *exceedingly* handsome.

CHAPTER THREE: PREPOSITIONS

Exercise 1:

Note that the following are example phrases. Your phrases will vary.

1. above the water **2.** after the bell tolled **3.** around the harbor **4.** at the neighbor's house **5.** behind the bleachers **6.** beneath the table **7.** between the dog and the cat **8.** down the winding slide **9.** during my teenage years **10.** from the potting shed **11.** into the haunted house **12.** off the island **13.** over the bridge **14.** throughout the movie **15.** toward the lighthouse **16.** until next week **17.** upon arrival **18.** within the school walls

Exercise 2:

Note that the following are example phrases. Your phrases will vary.

1. about the long book **2.** across the ancient bridge **3.** among well-known people **4.** beside an exquisite table **5.** beyond the long pier **6.** over the deep river **7.** past the obnoxious toll-keeper **8.** to the wild party **9.** underneath the blue house **10.** without annoying noises

Exercise 3:

1. Carrie is walking [into the room].
2. Dylan sits [on the chair].
3. The chair collapses [under Dylan].
4. Carrie is laughing [at Dylan].
5. Helga runs [to the kitchen] [from the bedroom].
6. Jessie's cousin swims [in the pond].
7. [After the shopping trip], Lucy was broke.
8. Lizzie is walking [on the path] [with her dog].
9. Jay's friend is going [to Phillips Academy].
10. Adrian is writing [in black ink].
11. [Before each performance], Pam gargles [with salt water].
12. The boy [from New Mexico] is traveling [into space].
13. Mr. Johnson is a professor [of mathematics] [at a prestigious university].
14. The CD is [on the desk] [in the bedroom].
15. [During periods] [of rain], Terry reads books [about cooking].

Exercise 4:

"It was quite late [in the evening] when the little Moss came snugly [to anchor], and Queequeg and I went ashore; so we could attend [to no business] that day, at least none [but a supper and a bed]. The landlord [of the Spouter Inn] had recommended us [to his cousin Hosea Hussey] [of the Try Pots], whom he asserted to be the proprietor [of one] [of the best kept hotels] [in all Nantucket], and moreover he had assured us that Cousin Hosea, [as he called him], was famous [for his chowders]. [In short], he plainly hinted that we could not possibly do better than try potluck [at the Try Pots]. But the directions he had given us [about keeping a yellow warehouse] [on our starboard hand] till we opened a white church [to the larboard], and then keeping that [on the larboard hand] till we made a corner three points [to the starboard], and that done, then ask the first man we met where the place was: these crooked directions [of his] very much puzzled us [at first], especially as, [at the outset], Queequeg insisted that the yellow warehouse--our first point [of departure]--must be left [on the larboard hand], whereas I had understood Peter Coffin to say it was [on the starboard]. However, [by dint] [of beating about a little] [in the dark], and now and then knocking up a peaceable inhabitant to inquire the way, we at last came [to something] which there was no mistaking."

Note: An argument could be made that the prepositional phrase "to anchor" in the first sentence is in fact an infinitive, a verb form that is discussed in detail in Chapter 8. However, to anchor" is commonly understood as shorthand for "to the place where we anchor," making it a prepositional phrase.

Exercise 5:

Note that the following are example sentences. Your sentences will vary.

1. Harry reads books [from the library] in order to save money.
2. Joel goes out [at night].
3. I like to go to temple [with my mother].
4. The bat found a way [into our attic].
5. After a moment [of hesitation], the pitcher gave a signal to the catcher.
6. The dog quickly maneuvered [through the crowd] and to its owner.
7. They store boxes in the space [under the stairs].
8. [During the exam], Haley could not stop sneezing.
9. "[Over the river], and through the woods" is a famous phrase from a Thanksgiving song.
10. I suggest you get your taxes done before April.

Exercise 6:

1. Sally is getting married [in New York City]. (adverb)
2. The eye [of the storm] is approaching. (adjective)
3. Jeff is going [to the movies]. (adverb)
4. The mother is putting gifts [under the Christmas tree]. (adverb)
5. This is a large portion [of pancakes]. (adjective)
6. Randy needs a key [for the front door]. (adjective)
7. Laura is hanging out [with friends]. (adverb)
8. The drawer [with the important files] is locked. (adjective)
9. The girl [with big ears] is listening. (adjective)
10. The girl is listening [with her big ears]. (adverb)

Exercise 7:

Note that the following are example sentences. Your sentences will vary.

1. The plasterboard under the wallpaper is crumbling.
2. The bug flew above her bed.
3. The cat jumped into the box.
4. The pillow with intricate stitching was sown by Debby.

5. The police tape around the house was taken down and stuffed in a garbage bag.
6. He always colors within the lines, even though he's only 5.
7. Nathan is known among his peers for his intelligence.
8. The space between the chairs and throughout the room will soon be filled with end tables and magazine racks.
9. Fiona kept quiet despite her bad temper.
10. The world beyond the horizon is just seeing sunrise now.

Exercise 8:

Note that the following are example sentences. Your sentences will vary.

1. The sand *along the shore* was littered with seaweed. (ADJ) I walked back and forth *along the shore*. (ADV)
2. The woman *across the river* is shouting at her boyfriend. (ADJ) The woman is shouting *across the river* to her boyfriend. (ADV)
3. The boy *between the girls* looked very uncomfortable. (ADJ) The boy is sitting *between the girls*. (ADV)
4. The meatballs *on the spaghetti* are enormous. (ADJ) I placed the meatballs *on the spaghetti* before serving it. (ADV)
5. The view *through the keyhole* was obstructed. (ADJ) I looked *through the keyhole* at the boys. (ADV)

Diagramming Exercises:

1. Sasha is kissing Joseph passionately under the mistletoe.

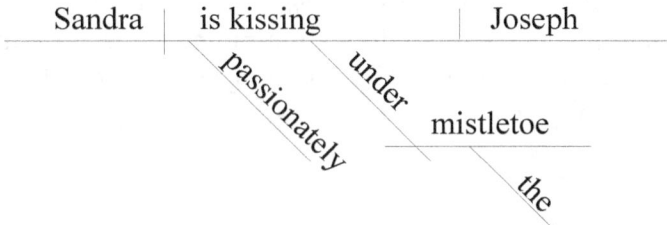

Under the mistletoe is a prepositional phrase acting as an adverb. We know it is adverbial because it tells us the location where the verb is taking place (*Where is Sasha kissing Joseph? Under the mistletoe.*). Then we can break the prepositional phrase into its parts; *under* is the preposition, *mistletoe* is the object of the preposition, and *the* is an article modifying *mistletoe*.

2. Kate approaches the pool without fear.

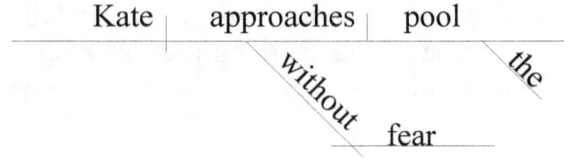

The prepositional phrase *without fear* is acting as an adverb because it tells us the manner in which Kate approaches the pool. *Without* is the preposition, and *fear* is its object.

3. Applications for college are quite daunting.

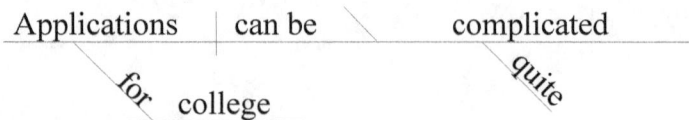

We must decide if the prepositional phrase *for college* is an adverb phrase or an adjective phrase. It tells us more information about the subject, *applications* (Applications for what? *For college.*), a noun, and so we know it is an adjective phrase modifying *applications*.

4. Silly children jump on a trampoline without any supervision.

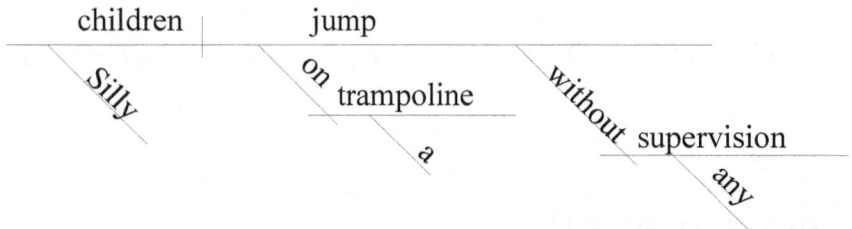

There are two prepositional phrases in this sentence: *on a trampoline* and *without any supervision*. Both tell us more about the way in which the children are jumping. *Where* are they jumping? *On a trampoline.* In what manner are they jumping? *Without any supervision.* Therefore, we diagram both phrases as adverb phrases modifying *jump*. This is an example of one verb being modified by more than one adverb phrase.

5. At night, teenagers throw wild parties in empty houses.

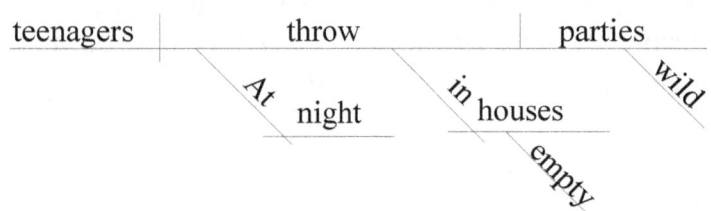

This sentence has two prepositional phrases: *at night* and *in empty houses*. *At night* tells us *when* the teenagers throw the parties, so we diagram the phrase as an adverb phrase. *In empty houses* tells us *where* the teenagers throw the parties, so we diagram this phrase as an adverb phrase as well.

6. Mimi bakes a chocolate cake for the mysterious man in the street.

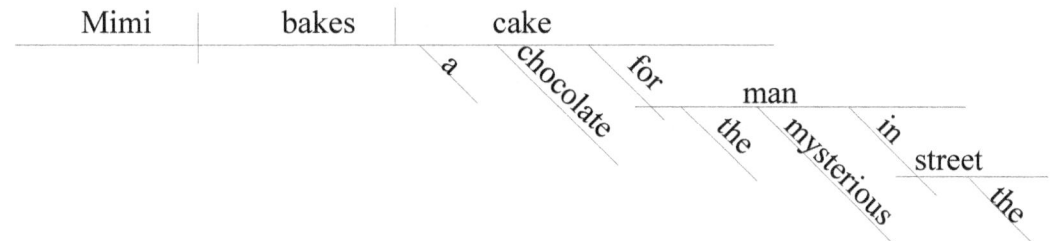

   We have two prepositional phrases to consider: *for the mysterious man* and *in the street*. *For the mysterious man* tells us more about the cake—Which cake? The cake *for the mysterious man*. Therefore, we diagram the phrase as an adjective modifying *cake*; remember that *the* and *mysterious* both modify the object of the preposition, *man*. *In the street* tells us more about the man, so we diagram the phrase as an adjective modifying *man*. Which man? The man *in the street*.

7. The surgeon is operating on the valves of the heart with great skill.

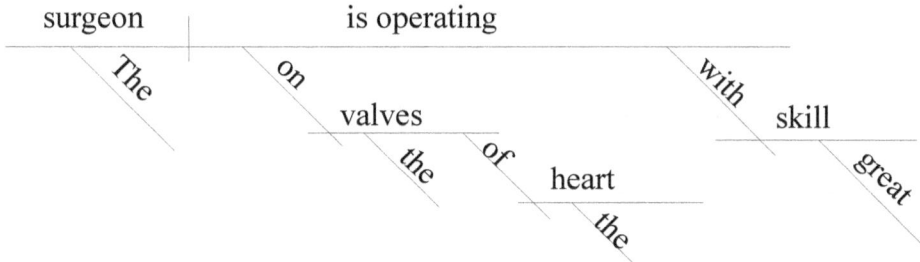

   We have three prepositional phrases in this sentence: *on the valves*, *of the heart*, and *with great skill*. *On the valves* tells us more about the verb *operating*—Operating on what? *On the valves*. *On the valves* is acting as an adverb modifying *is operating*. *Of the heart* tells us more about the valves, so it functions as an adjective. Which valves? The valves *of the heart*. *With great skill* also tells us more about the verb. *How* did the surgeon operate? *With great skill*.

8. The surgeon with great skill is operating on the valves of the heart.

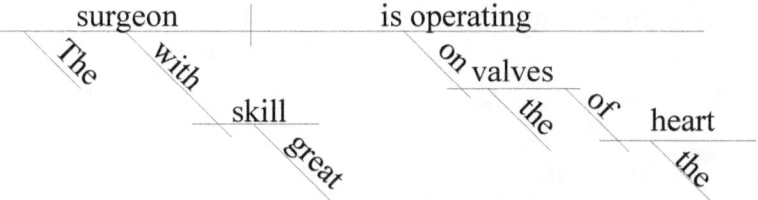

This sentence contains the exact same words as the sentence above it. However, the order in which the words appear is critical to a subtle difference between the sentences. Here the prepositional phrase *with great skill* had been moved from after *is operating on the valves of the heart* to after *the surgeon*. In the first sentence, we decided that *with great skill* was an adverb phrase, describing the manner in which the surgeon is operating. In this sentence, however, the same group of words is acting as an adjective phrase modifying *surgeon*—Which surgeon? The one *with great skill*.

9. Many people go to the beach in the month of July.

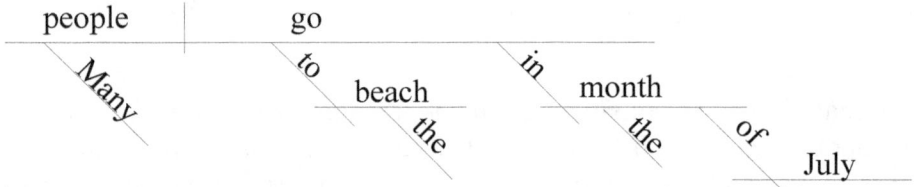

The prepositional phrases in this sentence are: *to the beach*, *in the month*, and *of July*. *To the beach* tells us more about the verb *go*—Where do people go? *To the beach*. Therefore, it is diagrammed as an adverb phrase. *In the month* also tells us more about *go*—When do people go to the beach? *In the month [of July]*. We diagram this phrase as an adverb as well. *Of July* then tells us more about the month—Which month? The month *of July*. Therefore, we diagram *of July* as an adjective phrase modifying month.

10. Does Jim have an answer to the difficult question?

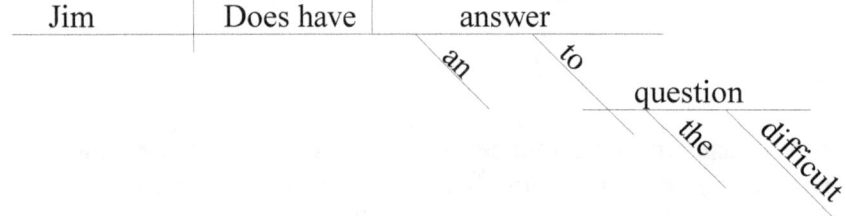

We have one prepositional phrase in this example: *to the difficult question*. This is an adjective phrase modifying *answer* because it answers the question: Which answer? The answer *to the difficult question*. *Question* is the object of the preposition *to*, and it is modified by *the* and *difficult*. *Does have* is a present emphatic verb.

11. The plane from Florida is landing at midnight tomorrow.

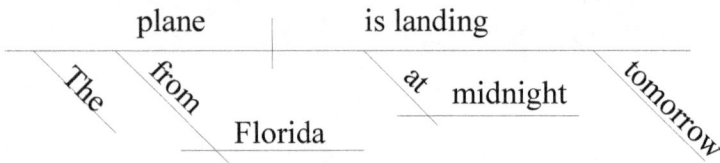

136

We have two prepositional phrases to diagram: *from Florida* and *at midnight*. *From Florida* tells us more about the plane: *Which* plane? The plane *from Florida*. Therefore we connect the phrase to *plane*. *At midnight*, on the other hand, tells us more about *is landing*. Like *tomorrow*, *at midnight* answers the question: *When* is the plane landing? We diagram it as an adverb modifying the verb.

12. Before the exam, Harriet quietly studies the notes in the hallway.

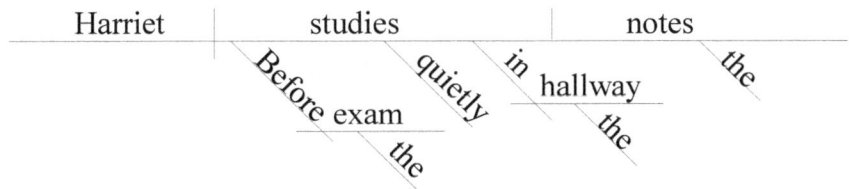

Our prepositional phrases are: *before the exam*, and *in the hallway*. *Before the exam* tells us more about the verb—*When* does Harriet study? *Before the exam*. We diagram *before the exam* as an adverb phrase modifying *studies*. *In the hallway* also tells us more about the verb—*Where* does Harriet study? *In the hallway*. Therefore we also diagram *in the hallway* as an adverb phrase.

13. The Trojans wheel the horse of those treacherous Greeks through the gates of the city.

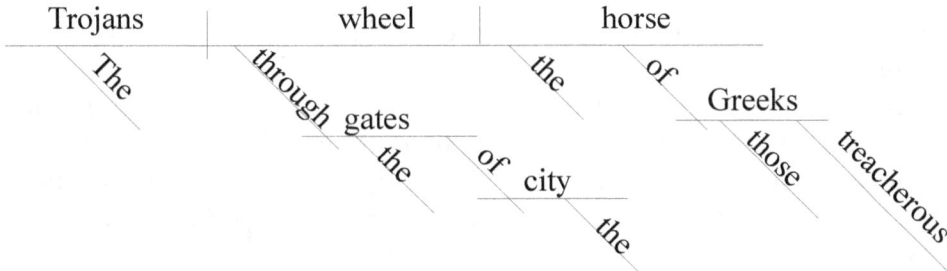

We must consider the following prepositional phrases: *through the gates*, *of the city*, and *of those treacherous Greeks*. *Through the gates* tells us more about the verb—*Where* do the Trojans wheel the horse? *Through the gates*. Therefore it is an adverb phrase. *Of the city* tells us more about the gates—*Which* gates? The gates *of the city*. *Of the Greeks* tells us more about the horse—*Which* horse? The horse *of those treacherous Greeks*. Both *of the city* and *of those treacherous Greeks* are adjective phrases, though they modify different nouns.

14. Throughout the summer, the Campbells visit the beautiful beaches of New England with friends.

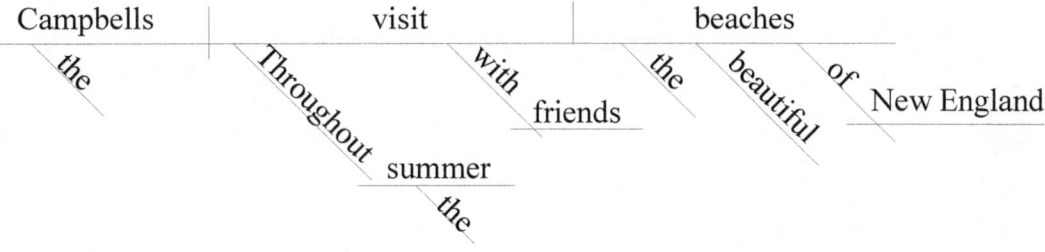

The prepositional phrases are: *throughout the summer*, *with friends*, and *of New England*. *Throughout the summer* tells us more about the verb—*When* do they visit the beaches? *Throughout the summer*. *With friends* also tells us more about the verb—*With whom* do they visit the beaches? *With friends*. Both phrases are adverb phrases. *Of New England*, on the other hand, tells us more about the beaches—*Which* beaches? The beaches *of New England*. *Of New England* is therefore an adjective phrase.

15. Celebrities in the sunny state of California live lavishly in some of the largest homes in the world.

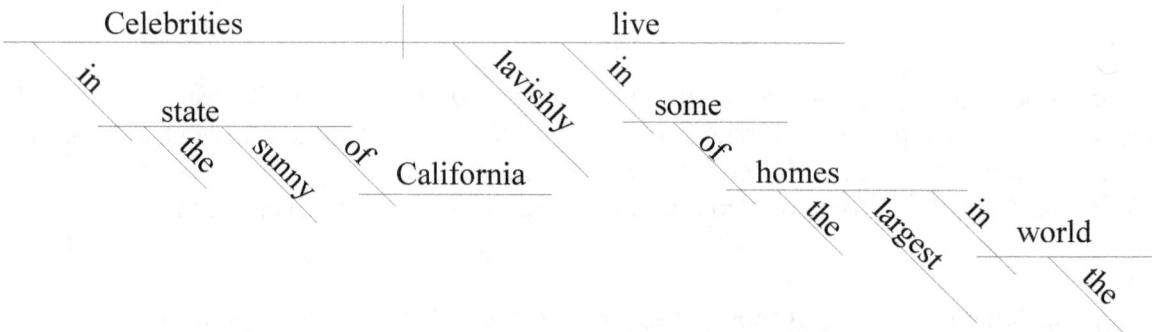

      This sentence is a true test of your mastery of prepositional phrases. Managing all the phrases in this sentence is not an easy task!
      Our prepositional phrases are: *in the sunny state; of California; in some; of the largest homes;* and *in the world*. Let's dissect this one phrase at a time. *In the sunny state* tells us more about *celebrities*—*Which* celebrities? The ones *in the sunny state*. Similarly, *of California* tells us more about *state*—*Which* state? The state *of California*. *In some* tells us more about *live*—*Where* do the celebrities live? *In some* [of the largest...]. *Of the largest homes* then tells us more about *some*—Some *of what*? Some *of the largest homes*. *In the world* then tells us more about *homes*—*Which* homes? *Homes in the world*. Systematically breaking the sentence down into its parts and figuring out which question each phrase answers helps us make sense of an otherwise overwhelming task.

Chapter Four: Pronouns

Exercise 1:

1. <u>His</u> brother is a brilliant student.
2. I am going on a date with <u>her</u> best friend.
3. That house is <u>theirs</u>.
4. <u>Your</u> dress is gorgeous!
5. I love everything about pizza, especially <u>its</u> aroma.
6. This jacket is <u>mine</u>, not <u>yours</u>.
7. They are washing <u>my</u> car with <u>their</u> buddies.

Exercise 2:

Note that the following are example sentences. Your sentences will vary.

1. *My* car was stolen.
2. That bag is *hers*.
3. *Their* dog is named Bo.
4. Is that jacket his or *yours*?
5. *Your* test is covered in eraser marks.
6. That packet is *ours*.

Exercise 3:

Note that the following are example sentences. Your sentences will vary.

1. He saw *himself* in the store window. (Reflexive). John *himself* scored the winning basket. (Intensive)
2. I hit *myself* by accident. (Reflexive). I *myself* supervised the project. (Intensive)
3. We watched *ourselves* in a home video. (Reflexive). We *ourselves* saw the robbery. (Intensive.)
4. You wrote *yourself* into the story. (Reflexive). You *yourself* drew the portrait. (Intensive)
5. You painted *yourselves* in self-portraits. (Reflexive). They *themselves* wrote the stories. (Intensive)

Exercise 4:

Note that the following are example sentences. Your sentences will vary.

1. *Who* knocked over the vase?
2. *What* test do you have to take?
3. *Which* form do you have to fill out?
4. For *whom* did you bake these cookies?
5. *Whose* dog is that?

Exercise 5:

1. I really want <u>that</u> puppy. (adjective)
2. <u>These</u> cookies have nuts in them. (adjective)
3. <u>Those</u> are my favorite colors. (pronoun)
4. <u>This</u> party is fantastic! (adjective)

5. <u>This</u> is a fantastic party! (pronoun)
6. She wants <u>this</u> dress and <u>these</u> shoes. (adjective; adjective)
7. <u>That</u> is truly unbelievable. (pronoun)
8. I never wear <u>this</u>. (pronoun)
9. Kendra is putting all <u>those</u> eggs in <u>this</u> basket. (adjective; adjective)
10. I prefer <u>these</u> cookies to <u>those</u>. (adjective; pronoun)

Exercise 6:

Note that the following are example sentences. Your sentences will vary.

1. I really want <u>another</u> cookie. (adjective) One commentator wanted McCain as president, while <u>another</u> wanted Obama. (pronoun)
2. <u>Neither</u> shirt looks good on you. (adjective) <u>Neither</u> fits you well. (pronoun)
3. May I have <u>more</u> cookies? (adjective) Some people dislike pizza; however, <u>more</u> love it. (pronoun)
4. With <u>each</u> turn, I get closer to winning the game. (adjective) Is getting a printer that can be connected to multiple computers better than buying one for <u>each</u>? (pronoun)
5. I don't have <u>much</u> free time. (adjective) She does <u>much</u> of her work at home. (pronoun)
6. There are <u>many</u> people at the town hall meeting. (adjective) <u>Many</u> of the shoes are too small. (pronoun)
7. Do you have <u>any</u> CDs by Oasis? (adjective) I didn't see <u>any</u>, did you? (pronoun)

Exercise 7:

1. Gretchen woke <u>herself</u> up for school at 6:30 a.m. (reflexive)
2. To <u>whom</u> are <u>you</u> referring? (interrogative; personal subjective)
3. Put <u>all</u> of the blame on <u>him</u>. (indefinite; personal objective)
4. Would <u>anybody</u> like to see a movie? (indefinite)
5. In <u>my</u> opinion, red cars look better than blue ones. (personal possessive)
6. <u>That</u>, <u>some</u> would say, is intolerable. (demonstrative; indefinite)
7. <u>He</u> did not know that <u>somebody</u> was approaching. (personal subjective; indefinite)
8. <u>Mine</u> are better than <u>yours</u>. (personal possessive; personal possessive)
9. John knew <u>them</u> better than <u>anyone</u>. (personal objective; indefinite)
10. Sheila scored the basket <u>herself</u>. (intensive)
11. <u>Whose</u> keys are <u>those</u>? (interrogative; demonstrative)
12. <u>Several</u> of the children dressed as witches on Halloween. (indefinite)
13. <u>Someone</u> on the school board leaked the agenda to the press. (indefinite)
14. When the cat saw <u>itself</u> in the mirror, <u>it</u> became very frightened. (reflexive; personal subjective)
15. Those documents are <u>mine</u>! Do not touch <u>them</u>! (personal possessive; personal objective)

Exercise 8:

Note that your answers may vary slightly than those given on some of the exercises.

1. Is Johnny speaking with <u>her</u>? (personal subjective)
2. Though <u>he</u> originally had doubted Pamela, Sam quickly began to trust <u>her</u>. (personal subjective; personal objective)
3. Did Greg throw away <u>his</u> old test papers? (personal possessive)

4. Time, <u>he</u> argues, is the fourth dimension. (personal subjective)
5. After <u>it</u> disappeared, <u>neither</u> of <u>them</u> noticed. (personal subjective; indefinite; personal objective)
6. Margaret asked <u>her</u> where it was that she was to drop off <u>her</u> forms. (personal objective; personal possessive)
7. Is <u>it</u> in your trunk? (personal subjective)
8. <u>Who</u> is knocking at my door? (interrogative)
9. Victoria <u>herself</u> won the race. (intensive)
10. <u>Some</u> of the protesters were wearing scarves. (indefinite)
11. <u>One</u> of the protesters was wearing a scarf. (indefinite)
12. <u>Which</u> of the protesters was wearing a scarf? (interrogative)
13. <u>What</u> kind of animal is this? (interrogative)
14. John congratulated <u>himself</u> when he won the prize. (reflexive)
15. Is that pen <u>mine</u>? (personal possessive)

Diagramming Exercises:

1. I am running.

```
     I    |   am running
```

I, the 1st person singular personal pronoun, is the subject of the sentence.

2. Does she need help?

```
    she   |  Does need  |  help
```

She, the 3rd person singular (feminine) personal pronoun, is the subject of the sentence. *Does need* is a present emphatic verb.

3. He is her friend.

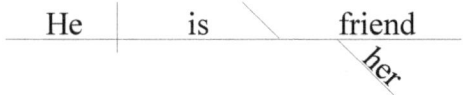

He, the 3rd person singular (masculine) personal pronoun, is the subject of the sentence. *Friend*, the predicate nominative, is modified by *her*, the feminine singular possessive pronoun.

4. You really want that.

You, the 2nd person singular personal pronoun, is the subject of the sentence. The demonstrative pronoun *that* is the direct object.

5. You really want that jacket.

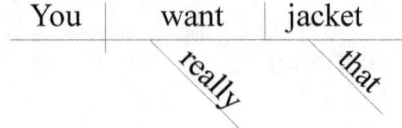

You, the 2nd person singular personal pronoun, is the subject. *Jacket,* the direct object, is modified by the demonstrative adjective (<u>not</u> pronoun) *that*.

6. Wanda wants both.

Wanda | wants | both

Both, an indefinite pronoun, is the direct object.

7. Wanda wants both kinds of cake.

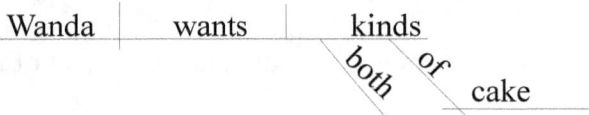

Here, *kinds* is the direct object, and *both* is acting as an adjective (<u>not</u> a pronoun) modifying *kinds*.

8. Is that man actually our new teacher?

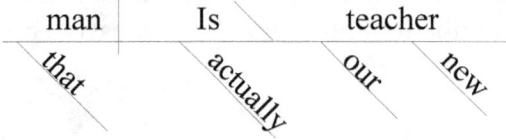

The demonstrative adjective *that* modifies *man*, and the possessive pronoun *our* modifies *teacher*.

9. You like his sister very much.

142

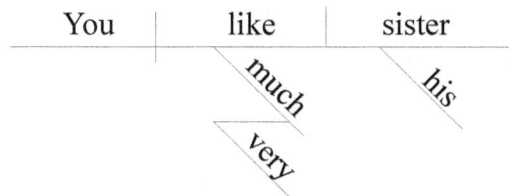

The personal pronoun *you* is the subject of the sentence. The possessive pronoun *his* modifies *sister*.

10. I am going to the new cafe around the corner with your big brother.

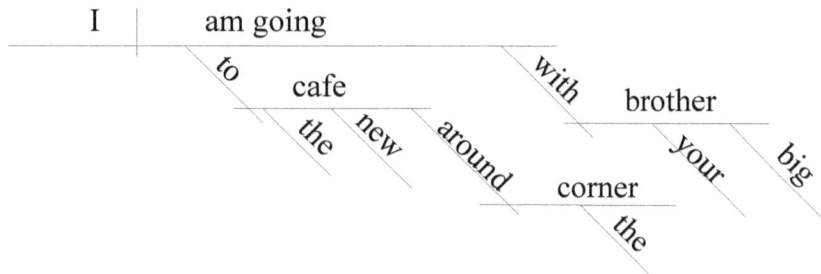

I, the 1st person singular personal pronoun, is the subject of the sentence. *Your* is a possessive pronoun (2nd person—whether it's singular or plural is actually ambiguous) modifying *brother*.

11. In the cozy corner, they are reading books aloud to us.

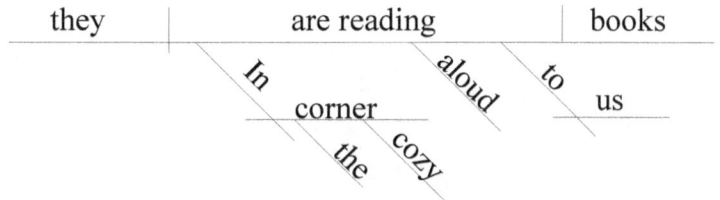

The personal pronoun *they*, the 3rd person plural, is the subject of the sentence. *To us* is an adverb phrase; *us*, the objective form of the 1st person plural personal pronoun, is the object of the preposition *to*.

12. I am willingly lending them your car for the rest of their vacation.

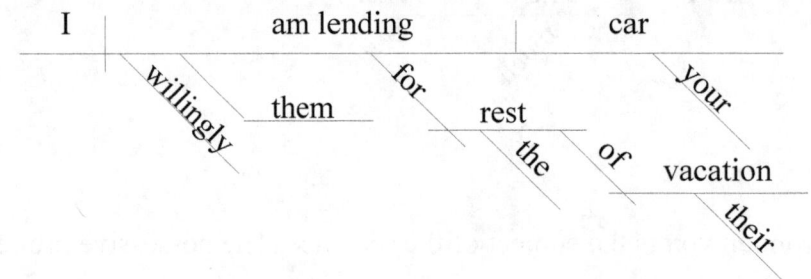

Car, the direct object, is modified by the possessive pronoun *your*—2nd person, but again, plural or singular is unclear. *Them*, the object form of the 3rd person plural personal pronoun, is the indirect object. *Their*, the 3rd person plural possessive pronoun, modifies *vacation*.

CHAPTER FIVE: MORE ABOUT VERBS

Exercise 1:

1. It <u>might have</u> *been* wise to work hard in high school.
2. You <u>should have</u> *foreseen* having your finger injured after <u>having</u> placed it under the lawn mower.
3. I <u>have</u> never *seen* such motivation in a child.
4. To persist <u>may</u> not necessarily *be* to prevail.
5. You <u>could have</u> *saved* money by switching to Geico.
6. Bobbie <u>may</u> still *catch* the train if he leaves now.
7. <u>Had</u> you *attended* college, you <u>might be</u> *making* more money now.
8. If you weren't so unsure of yourself, you <u>might</u> *be* more willing to try new things.
9. Catherine <u>could</u> not *understand* why Robert <u>didn't</u> *find* her attractive.
10. Alex <u>had</u> *shown* up late to work too many times, so his boss fired him.
11. If I <u>had</u> *used* the copier, I <u>might have</u> *saved* much time.
12. You <u>should have</u> *chosen* the apple since you are very hungry.   13. What <u>could have</u> possibly *caused* the problem?
14. He <u>could have</u> *been* a scientist if he <u>had</u> *wanted* to; she <u>could</u> not. (The third helping verb, *could*, refers back to and implies the main verb *been* and its helping verb, have: "She could not have been.")
15. They <u>were</u> *celebrating* Thanksgiving with a large feast last year.

Exercise 2:

1. Future **2.** Past **3.** Present **4.** Past **5.** Future **6.** Present **7.** Present **8.** Present **9.** Future **10.** Past

Exercise 3:

1. Future Progressive **2.** Past Progressive **3.** Future Progressive **4.** Present Progressive **5.** Present Progressive **6.** Future Progressive **7.** Past Progressive **8.** Present Progressive **9.** Past Progressive **10.** Future Progressive

Exercise 4:

Note that the following are example sentences. Your sentences will vary.

1. He is walking to school. (present progressive); I was walking to school when I saw a dog chase a car. (past progressive) You will be walking to school. (future progressive)
2. We are trying to win. (present progressive) You were trying to win, but we beat you. (past progressive) They will be trying to win when we compete against them. (future progressive)
3. I am baking cookies. (present progressive) We were baking cookies for the bake sale. (past progressive) She will be baking for the next bake sale. (future progressive)

Exercise 5:

1. Present Perfect **2.** Past Perfect **3.** Present Perfect **4.** Future Perfect **5.** Past Perfect **6.** Future Perfect **7.** Present Perfect **8.** Past Perfect **9.** Future Perfect **10.** Present Perfect

Exercise 6:

Note that the following are example sentences. Your sentences will vary.

1. She has lived in Switzerland for three years. (present perfect) I had lived in Austria before moving to Germany. (past perfect) You will have lived a full life. (future perfect)
2. They have explored many odd places. (present perfect) I had explored the cave before, but this time I found bats hibernating there. (past perfect) We will have explored many countries by the time we return from sabbatical. (future perfect)
3. He has learned many things in college. (present perfect). I had learned some odd facts during my studies at the Pike school. (past perfect) You will have learned discipline by the time you complete basic training. (future perfect)

Exercise 7:

1. Past Perfect **2.** Future Perfect Progressive **3.** Future Perfect Progressive **4.** Past Perfect Progressive **5.** Present Perfect Progressive **6.** Past Perfect Progressive **7.** Present Perfect Progressive **8.** Future Perfect Progressive **9.** Past Perfect Progressive **10.** Future Perfect Progressive

Exercise 8:

Note that the following are example sentences. Your sentences will vary.

1. I have been building a birdhouse. (present perfect progressive) He had been building a clock, but it fell apart. (past perfect progressive) We will have been building our savings for 30 years by the time we retire. (future perfect progressive)
2. They have been gardening. (present perfect progressive) You had been gardening for a while. (past perfect progressive) She will have been gardening. (future perfect progressive)
3. He has been looking over here. (present perfect progressive) We had been looking at the art exhibit. (past perfect progressive) On Feb. 1, you will have been looking for a job for more than a year. (future perfect progressive)

Exercise 9:

1. Past Perfect **2.** Future Perfect **3.** Present Perfect Progressive **4.** Future Perfect Progressive **5.** Present Progressive **6.** Past Perfect Progressive **7.** (Simple) Future **8.** Past Progressive **9.** Future Progressive **10.** Present Perfect **11.** (Simple) Present **12.** (Simple) Past **13.** Past Perfect Progressive **14.** Future Progressive **15.** Future Perfect **16.** Present Perfect **17.** Past Perfect **18.** Present Progressive **19.** Future Perfect Progressive **20.** Past Progressive **21.** Past Perfect **22.** (Simple) Present **23.** (Simple) Past **24.** (Simple) Future

Exercise 10:

Note that your active sentences may vary slightly than those given on some of the exercises.

1. Active
2. Passive: *They consumed dozens of hotdogs as well.*
3. Passive: *Pilgrims founded this country.*
4. Active
5. Passive: *A larger and more athletic team crushed ours.*

6. Active
7. Passive: *A lumberjack from a neighboring town found the missing child.*
8. Passive: *A large investment firm in New York employed the man.*
9. Active
10. Passive: *A few years ago, a car struck Stephen King, the author of numerous best sellers.*
11. Passive: *One of the summer interns lost the papers.*
12. Passive: *The teacher spilled Wite-Out all over the table.*
13. Active
14. Passive: *Our teacher tested us on all the new material.*
15. Passive: *The tornado flattened thousands of cornstalks.*
16. Passive: *He ordered the hot chocolate without whipped cream.*
17. Active
18. Passive: *My dog broke the coat rack before I returned home.*
19. Passive: *High winds crushed the trees during the thunderstorm.*
20. Active
21. Active
22. Passive: *The tidal wave devastated the island's people.*
23. Passive: *A masked man robbed the store.*
24. Active
25. Passive: *The cleaning crew vacuumed the floor yesterday.*
26. Active
27. Passive: *The police broke up the rowdy party.*
28. Passive: *George Lucas wrote, directed and produced* Star Wars.

CHAPTER 6: CONJUNCTIONS, INTERJECTIONS, AND DIRECT ADDRESS

Exercise 1:

1. Mr. Thompson is a math teacher *and* a soccer coach at the high school.
2. Jonah skied in the Alps over Christmas break *and* had a great time.
3. Tom has traveled to England, *but* he has never gone to France.
4. The coffee is too hot, *so* I will drink it lukewarm.
5. Tony wants to order shrimp scampi *and* steak, *but* he doesn't have room for both.
6. I would eat rice, *but* not potatoes.
7. We could cook dinner, *or* we could just order Chinese takeout.
8. He needs to study a lot for this test, *or* he will fail the class.

Exercise 2:

1. or 2. whether 3. nor 4. and 5. but also

Diagramming Exercises:

1. Christine is both extremely intelligent and intensely beautiful.

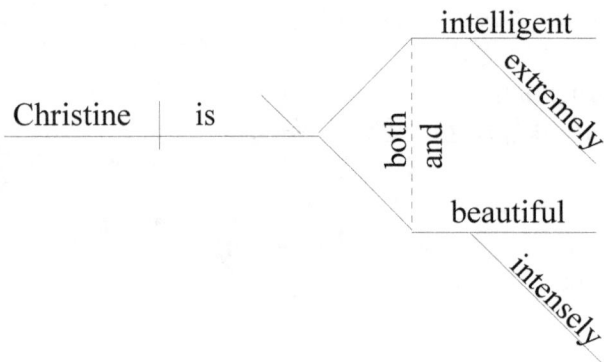

    Both intelligent and beautiful is a compound predicate adjective connected by the correlative conjunctions *both...and*. Each adjective is modified is modified by an adverb (*extremely* and *intensely*).

2. Kelly and Kyle are having coffee and cookies on their porch.

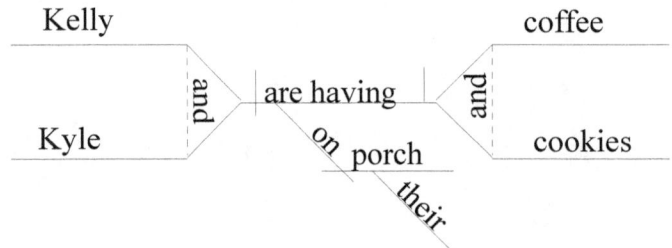

Kelly and Kyle is a compound subject joined by the coordinating conjunction *and*. *Coffee and cookies* is a compound object, also joined by *and*.

3. Neither Mrs. Plunkett nor Mr. Redman buys fancy clothes or is tall and thin.

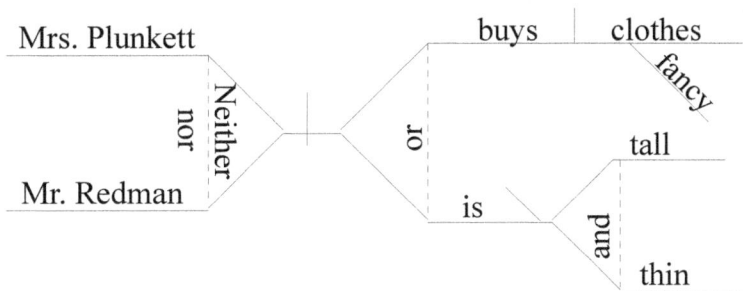

This sentence has both a compound subject (*Neither Mrs. Plunkett nor Mr. Redman*) and a compound predicate (the word *predicate* refers to everything that is separate from the subject and not an independent element). The predicate includes the linking verb *is*, a singular verb because although the subject is compound, it is not plural (*neither/nor* and *either/or* always take singular verbs, while a compound subject joined by *and* takes a plural verb). The first predicate, *buys fancy clothes*, is an action verb and a direct object. The second predicate, *is tall and thin*, is a linking verb with a compound predicate adjective (*tall and thin*).

4. Does this boy live in a city in Texas or in a suburb in California?

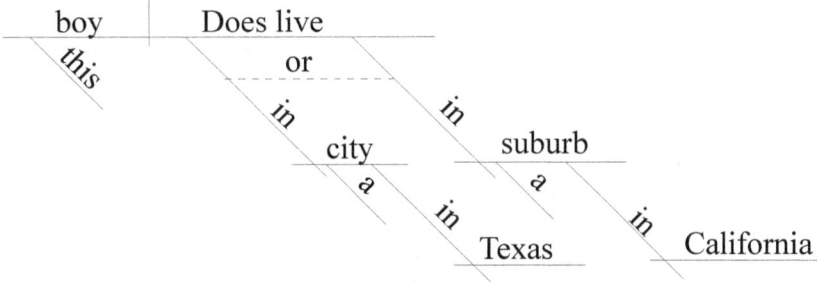

The verb *does live* is modified by the compound prepositional phrase *in a city or in a suburb*. The coordinating conjunction *or* joins the prepositional phrases. *In Texas* modifies *city*, and *in California* modifies *suburb*.

5. Either Jimmy or Julia will come through the door and into the room, but the other will not come.

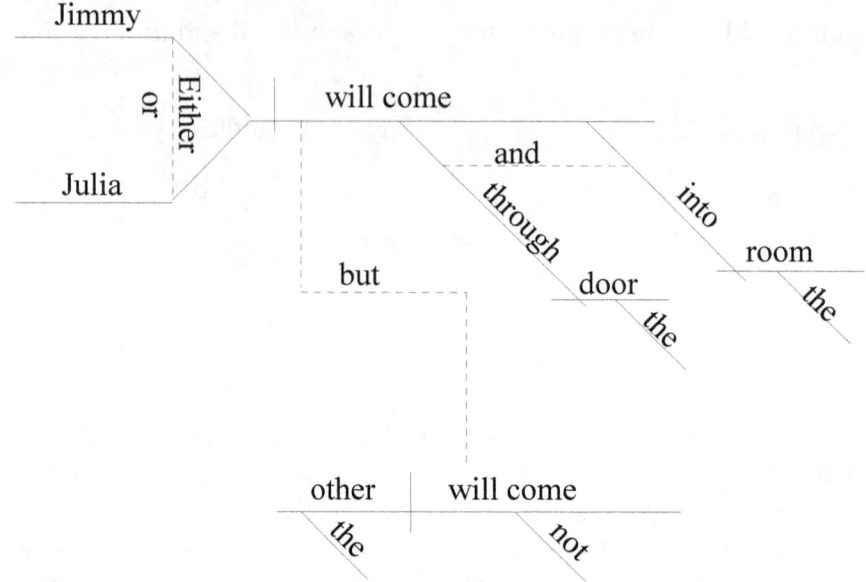

Either Jimmy or Julia is a compound subject taking a singular verb. *Through the door and into the room* is a compound prepositional phrase. The coordinating conjunction *but* joins the two separate ideas, or independent clauses (meaning each has a subject and a verb), making this a compound sentence. *Not* is an adverb.

6. They walked for several years through hot deserts and gloomy forests, and they finally came to their homeland.

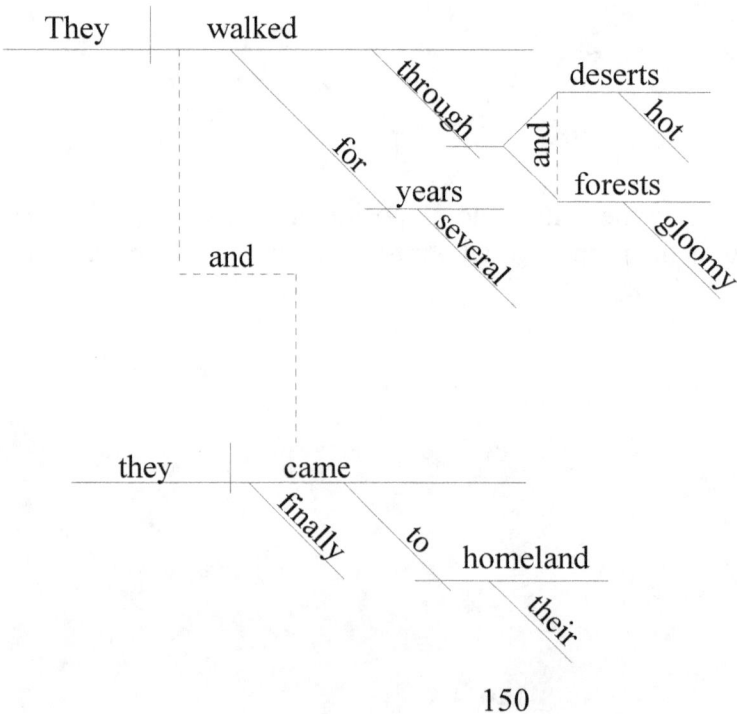

Deserts and forests is a compound object of a preposition. *Hot* modifies *deserts*, and *gloomy* modifies *forests*. *And* connects the independent clause *they finally came to their homeland* to the first part of the sentence, making this a compound sentence. *Finally* is an adverb.

7. Our team has passion, dedication, and desire, but their team has neither heart nor soul.

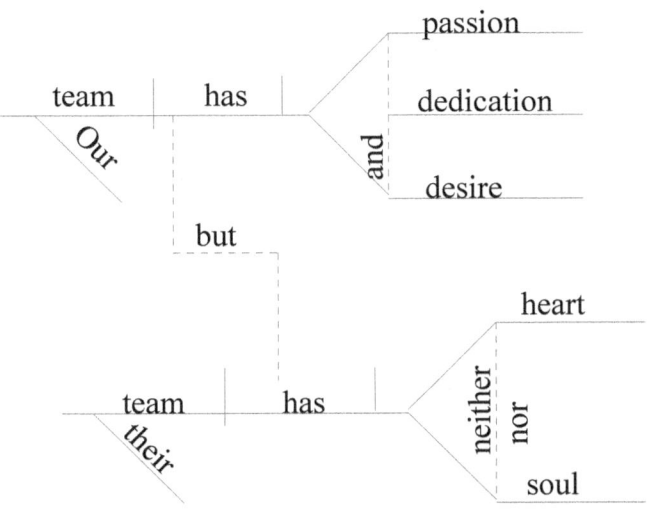

The first part of this compound sentence has a compound direct object. *And* is placed off-center according to its placement in the series of the three direct objects. The second part of the compound sentence also has a compound direct object, but there are two, not three, direct objects, and they are connected by correlative conjunctions, not a coordinating conjunction.

8. Every student in the group not only participated in the discussion, but also worked tirelessly and passionately.

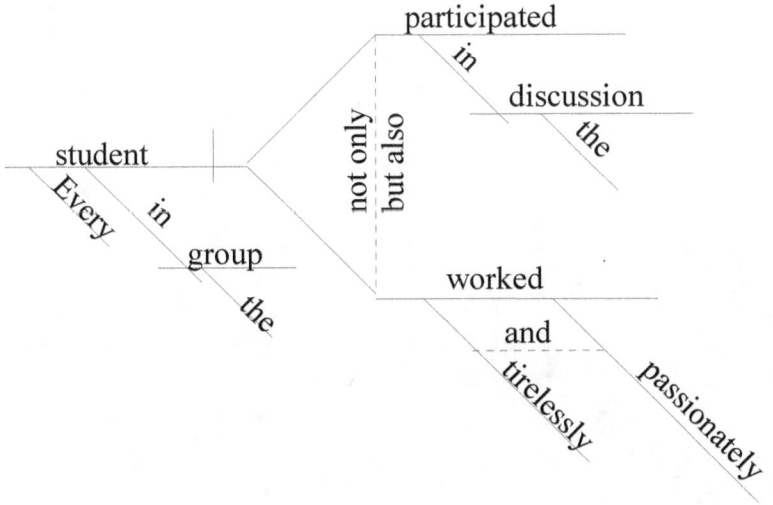

151

This sentence contains a compound predicate (everything coming after the subject) connected by correlative conjunctions (*not only...but also*). The second of the two predicates, *worked tirelessly and passionately*, contains a compound adverb.

9. How many cookies did he eat and from whom did he get them?

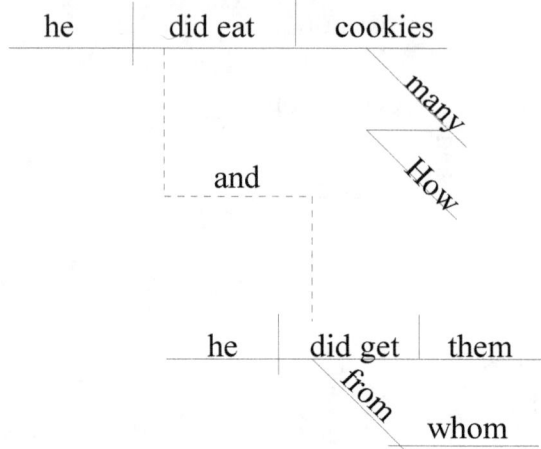

This is a compound sentence. Each of its two parts has the pronoun *he* as its subject and a direct object (*cookies*, *them*). *Many* is an adjective modifying *cookies*, and *how* is an adverb modifying *many*. The interrogative pronoun *whom* is the object of the preposition *from*.

Chapter 7: Verbals and Phrases

Exercise 1:

1. Mr. Smith, [the baker], wakes up at 6 a.m. every morning.
2. I would like to be friends with Ashley and Veronica, [two very popular girls in our class].
3. My pal [Miranda] loves going shopping with me.
4. Josh Beckett, [tonight's starting pitcher for the Red Sox], has an impressive record.
5. The Oscar-winning actor [Sean Penn] will be making an appearance.
6. Sophocles, [author of many ancient Greek tragedies], died at the age of ninety.
7. Former Hawaiian senator [Daniel Akaka] is a member of the Democratic Party.
8. Grammar, [a subject typically despised by young students], is easy to learn with this book, [an engaging compilation of examples and exercises].

Exercise 2:

Note that the following are example sentences. Your sentences will vary.

1. Jackie, my cousin from Texas, is an aspiring actress.
2. My sister, a skilled athlete, has always motivated me to stay fit.
3. We're buying a gift for our friend Kathryn.
4. At the restaurant, Paul will order his favorite dessert, chocolate chip ice cream.
5. Nail-biting, my biggest pet peeve, is disgusting to watch.
6. Terry had to run away from Spike, his next-door neighbors' dog.
7. The graduates eagerly awaited the address of the keynote speaker, a noted author.
8. George, the treasurer of the student council, stood up to make an announcement.

Exercise 3:

1. The chef, <u>baking</u> a cake, stirred the frosting. (present active)
2. The <u>silenced</u> crowd watched in awe. (past passive)
3. The boy <u>running</u> by my house waved hello. (present active)
4. <u>Having changed</u> her mind, Lara turned and ran the other way. (past active)
5. The girl, <u>driving</u> her car, made a wrong turn. (present active)
6. Lisa noticed the boy <u>singing</u> a song. (present active)
7. John, <u>having eaten</u> half the apple, noticed a <u>wriggling</u> worm inside. (past active; present active)
8. <u>Having said</u> goodbye to my friends and family, I boarded the <u>awaiting</u> plane. (past active, present active)
9. The <u>shimmering</u> comet rose higher into the sky until it was above the <u>mesmerized</u> crowd. (present active; past passive)
10.. The <u>reheated</u> meal was eaten by the girl. (past passive)
11. Mr. Hobart, <u>teaching</u> a class, called on the girl <u>sitting</u> in the back. (present active; present active)

Exercise 4:

1. the *barking* dog 2. the *frozen* yogurt 3. the *swimming* boy 4. the *shining* star 5. the *purring* cat 6. the *croaking* frog 7. the *shuttered* store 8. the apple, *having been infested by a worm* 9. the girl, *having eaten ten apple pies* 10. the car, *painted red*

Exercise 5:

1. Being **2.** Written **3.** Finding **4.** Chewed **5.** Walking **6.** Devastated **7.** Scanning **8.** Composed

Exercise 6:

1. Pamela enjoys [playing softball].
2. [Eating pizza and ice cream every day] isn't healthy.
3. Charlie evaded punishment by [lying about his misdemeanors].
4. [Watching movies] makes me sleepy.
5. She loves [strolling through the park with her best friends].
6. [Dissecting earthworms] is quite fascinating.
7. [Speaking in Pig Latin] becomes boring very quickly.
8. [My baby's constant crying] is distressing me.
9. I love [speaking in foreign languages].
10. [Winning] is quite rewarding.

Exercise 7:

Note that the following are example sentences. Your sentences will vary.

1. My family goes to New Hampshire every winter for *skiing* and snowboarding.
2. *Running* a mile is an impossible task for me!
3. Ella passes her summer days by *reading* thick novels while lying in a hammock.
4. *Eating* more fruits and vegetables helped Jocelyn lose weight.
5. Lenny hates *swimming* in saltwater.
6. *Playing* with friends makes snow days a joy!
7. By *flying* to New York instead of driving, I will arrive sooner.
8. Philosophers focus on *contemplating* the meaning of life.

Exercise 8:

Note that the following are example sentences. Your sentences will vary.

1. Looking up words in the dictionary is the best way to understand their meaning and use.
2. Researching on a computer makes writing history papers much easier.
3. Spellchecking carelessly will lead to an essay full of silly mistakes.
4. Many drivers are distracted by talking on their cell phones.
5. I much prefer eating slowly to bolting my meals.
6. My sister's singing in the shower prevents me from falling asleep each night.

Exercise 9:

Note that the following are example sentences. Your sentences will vary.

1. Chewing gum gives Georgina a terrible headache.
2. Mrs. Jenson, a professional chef, loves baking cookies for her family and friends.
3. My least favorite household chore is cleaning the kitchen.

4. Breathing slowly and deeply can relieve stress.
5. We passed the afternoon by trying on shoes in the department store.
6. Diane likes taking out the garbage.

Exercise 10:

1. swimming (P); covered (P) **2.** ringing (G) **3.** crowning (G) **4.** having been embarrassed (P); answering (G) **5.** swinging (G) **6.** having seen (P) **7.** reveling (P); winning (G) **8.** thinking (G) **9.** having written (P); publishing (G) **10.** playing (G)

Exercise 11:

Note that the following are example sentences. Your sentences will vary.

1. Peggy got that bruise by skating in the street without knee pads. (skating = gerund)
2. Having eaten two pieces of pie and three scoops of ice cream, Harrison felt sick to his stomach. (having eaten = participle)
3. Exercising frequently is the only way to get in shape. (exercising = gerund)
4. My brother, hearing my scream from the other room, ran to help me. (hearing = participle)
5. Reading many different genres will improve your own writing. (reading = gerund; writing = gerund)
6. Running a victory lap after winning the race, William tripped over his shoelace. (running = participle; winning = gerund)
7. Having flown in through the open door and bitten me several times, the mosquito slipped out unnoticed. (having flown = participle; (having) bitten = participle)
8. Looking in all the wrong places makes finding things very difficult. (looking = gerund; finding = gerund)

Diagramming Exercises:

1. Joan, a musician, loves flying with her family.

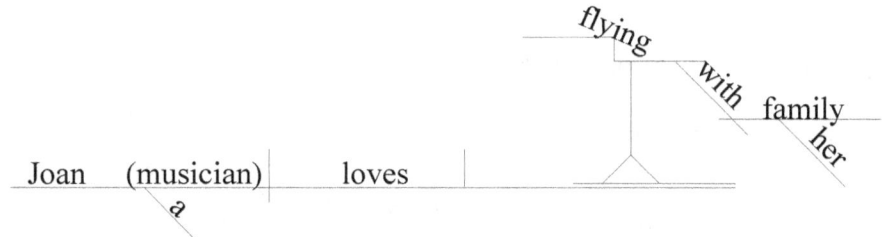

    Musician is in apposition with *Joan*. *Flying* is a gerund, a verbal noun. Here, *flying* is functioning as the direct object. *With her family* is a prepositional phrase that modifies the <u>verbal</u> part of the gerund, so we place it on the lower line of the gerund "step."

2. Looking at the passing clouds, I saw the shape of a dragon.

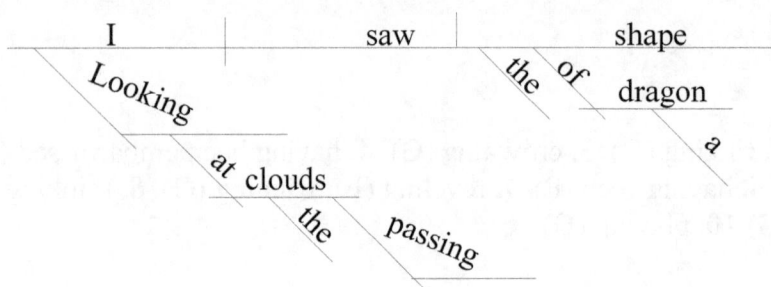

Looking at the passing clouds is a participial phrase modifying the subject, *I*. *Passing*, like *looking*, is a present active participle; it modifies *clouds*.

3. An excess of earwax blocked his hearing.

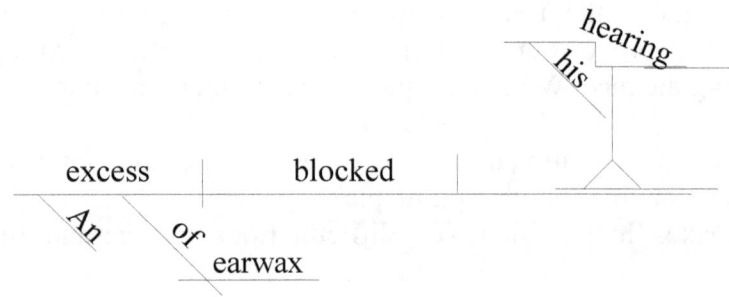

The gerund *hearing* is the sentence's direct object; the noun part of *hearing* is modified by *his*, so we place *his* on the upper portion of the step.

4. I escaped the barking dog by jumping over the fence.

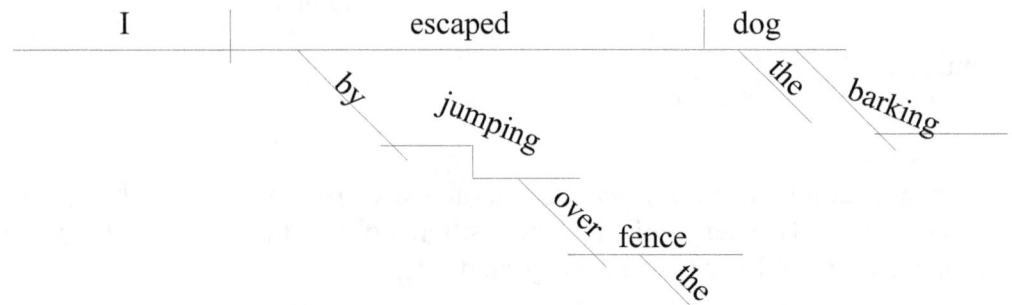

The participle *barking* modifies the sentence's direct object, *dog*. The gerund *jumping* is the object of the preposition *by*. *Over the fence* modifies the verbal part of the gerund, so we diagram it coming off of the lower portion of the step.

5. Reading well is a very important skill for high school.

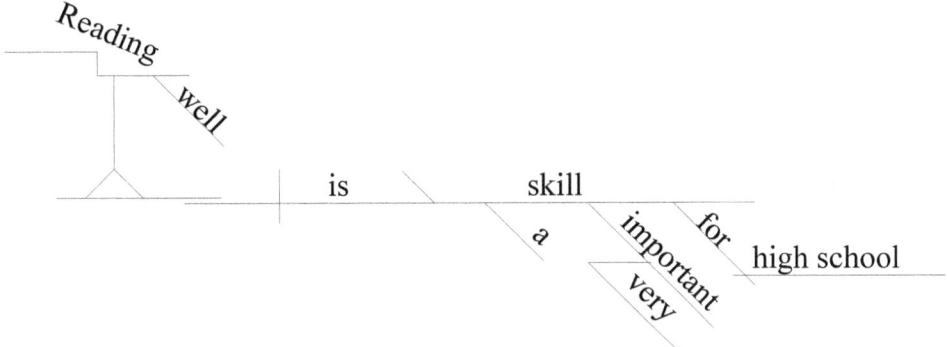

The subject of this sentence is the gerund *reading*. The adverb *well* modifies the verbal part of the gerund. *Very* is an adverb modifying the adjective *important*.

6. The girl, crimping her hair, dropped the hot iron onto the floor of her bathroom.

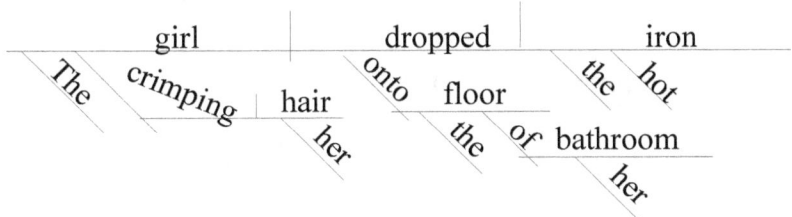

Crimping is a present active participle modifying the subject, *girl*. *Onto the floor* is an adverbial prepositional phrase.

7. Walking around the street on a hot day, I bumped into my neighbor carrying his groceries.

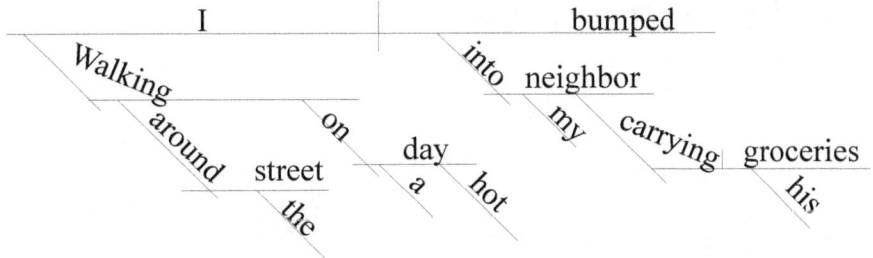

The subject, *I*, is modified by the present active participle *walking*. The present active participle *carrying* modifies *neighbor*, the object of the preposition *into*.

8. Carrying his groceries, I bumped into my neighbor walking around the street on a hot day.

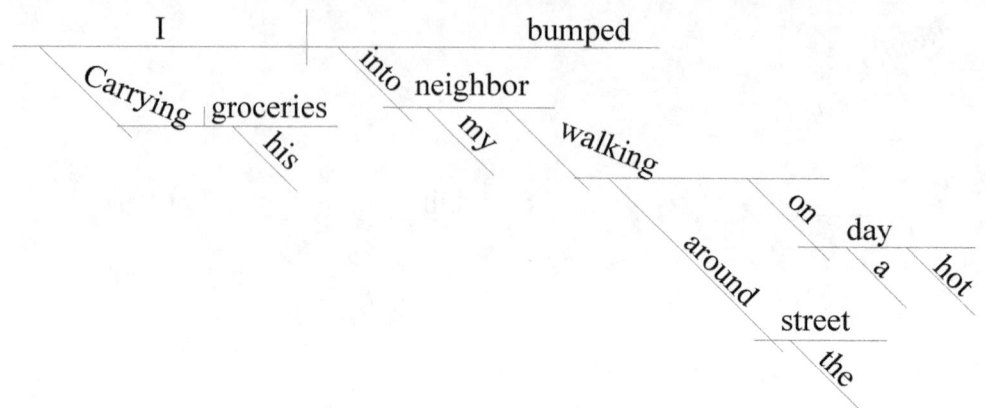

    This sentence contains all the same words as the sentence above, but the participle phrases are switched to modify different nouns. Here, *carrying his groceries* modifies *I*, meaning that our fictional *I* is carrying his neighbor's groceries for some reason. *Walking* now modifies *neighbor*.

9. Kelly, the woman painting my nails, is telling me a story about gardening.

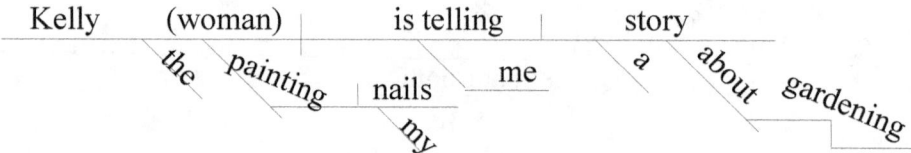

    The woman painting my nails is in apposition with *Kelly*. Within that appositive phrase, *painting* is a participle taking the direct object *nails*. The prepositional phrase *about gardening* modifies story; *gardening* is a gerund.

10. Several people kept gawking at the burning house.

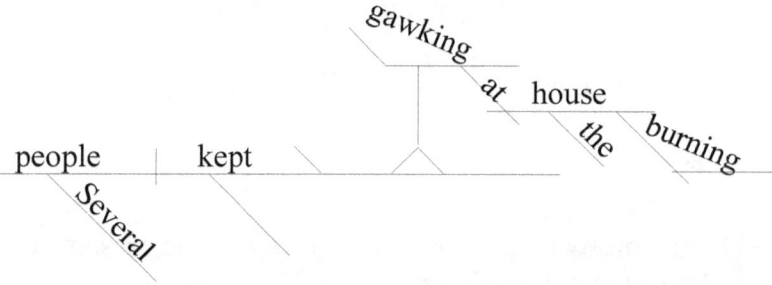

    Here, *kept* is acting as a linking verb. *Gawking* introduces a participial phrase functioning as a predicate adjective. *Burning* is another participle; it modifies *house*.

11. Having read the offensive letter written by the CEO angered by the terrible work of his lazy employees, I promptly quit my job.

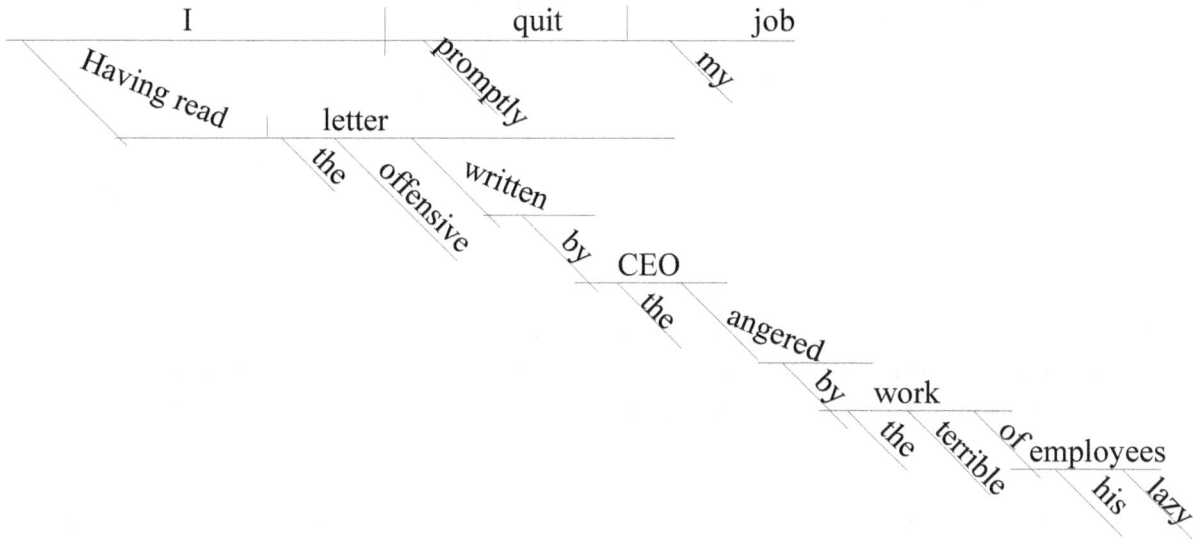

The past active participle *having read* modifies the subject, *I*. The past passive participle *written* (short for *having been written*) modifies *letter*, the direct object of the previous participle. *Angered* (short for *having been angered*), another past passive participle, modifies *CEO*.

12. A book, autographed by its famous author, was sitting on the counter.

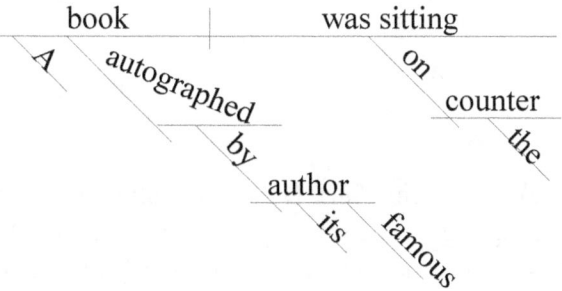

Autographed is a past passive participle (short for *having been autographed*) modifying the subject, *book*. *By its famous author* is a prepositional phrase modifying the participle.

13. Having been spotted in the crowd by throngs of her adoring fans, the celebrity was surrounded by a circle of guards protecting her safety.

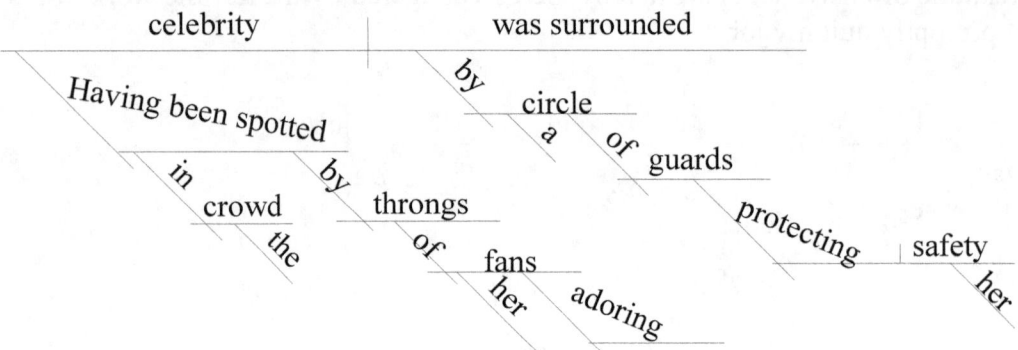

Having been spotted is a past passive participle modifying the subject, *celebrity*. *Adoring* is a present active participle modifying *fans*, the object of a preposition. *Protecting* is another present active participle; it modifies *guards*, the object of a preposition.

14. Lila, fascinated by studying ancient cultures, visited decaying ruins throughout South America.

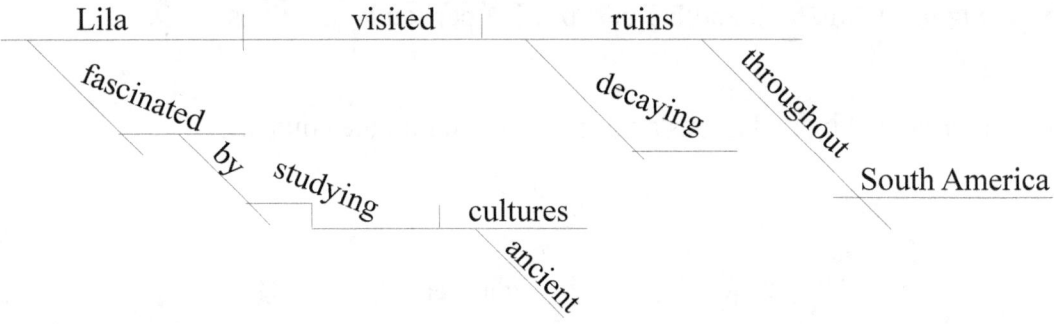

Fascinated is a participle (past passive) modifying *Lila*. By what is she fascinated? *By studying*. This is a prepositional phrase containing a gerund, *studying*, as the object of the preposition. *Cultures* is the object of the verbal part of the gerund *studying*. The participle (present active) *decaying* modifies *ruins*. The prepositional phrase *throughout South America* also modifies *ruins*.

15. My extremely lazy son should clean his bedroom without my asking.

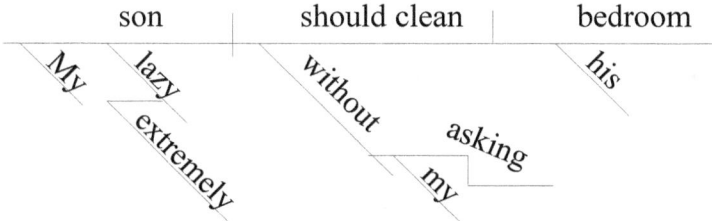

Without my asking is a prepositional phrase modifying *should clean*. The gerund *asking* is being used as the object of a preposition. The adjective *my* modifies the noun part of the gerund, and so it is diagrammed on the upper portion of the step.

16. My being reprimanded for my misdeeds will change my attitude about behaving badly.

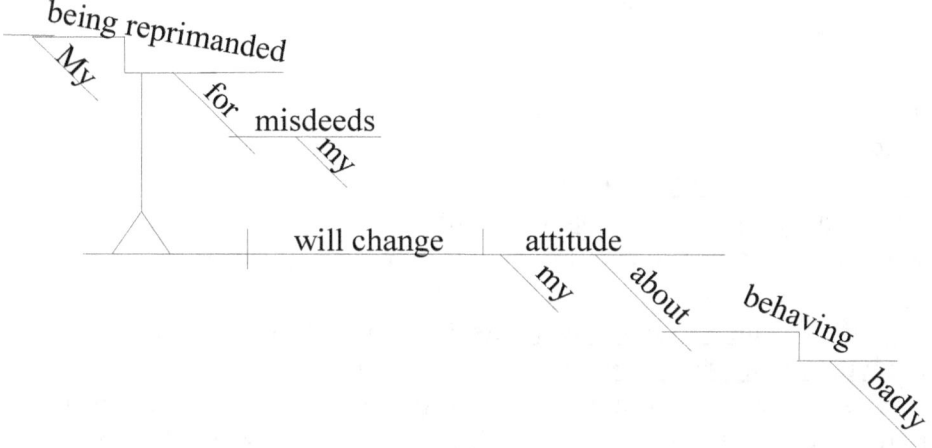

The gerund phrase *my being reprimanded for my misdeeds* is the subject of the sentence. The initial adjective *my* modifies the noun part of the gerund (*being reprimanded*), but the prepositional phrase *for my disdeeds* modifies the verbal part of the geund. *Attitude*, the direct object of the sentence, is modified by the prepositional phrase *about behaving badly*. *Behaving*, the object of the preposition, is a gerund, and the adverb *badly* modifies the verbal part of the gerund.

Chapter 8: Infinitives

Exercise 1:

Note that the following are example sentences. Your sentences will vary.

1. I would like to talk to the store's manager.
2. Can we agree to disagree?
3. Alana is too health-conscious to eat junk food all the time.
4. The shopkeeper is going to make you an offer on that necklace.
5. My ability to hear quiet sounds has diminished over the years.
6. That girl is much too intelligent to be in middle school!
7. Jesse refuses to make his bed.
8. David wants to leave the baseball game before the ninth inning.

Exercise 2:

1. <u>To be dishonest in school</u> is a problem. (noun)
2. It is too hard <u>to chew</u>. (adverb)
3. The day <u>to begin college</u> had arrived. (adjective)
4. This urge <u>to pick my nose</u> is overwhelming. (adjective)
5. It is difficult <u>to resist</u>. (adverb)
6. I would love <u>to visit the Dead Sea sometime</u>. (noun)
7. Ronnie would sacrifice anything <u>to be a rock star</u>. (adverb)
8. My father put a mousetrap in the garage <u>to capture that pesky rodent</u>. (adverb)
9. One way <u>to annoy your sister</u> would be <u>to put frogs in her bed</u>. (adjective; noun)
10. <u>To avoid running into that arrogant football player</u> was the only thing on her mind. (noun)
11. <u>To jump out of a plane without any safety gear</u> is insane. (noun)
12. Knights in medieval times always wore armor in battle <u>to protect themselves</u>. (adverb)
13. Many people learn <u>to read</u> very early in life, because reading is an important skill <u>to have</u>. (noun; adjective)
14. <u>To volunteer at a charity</u> is generous, although many people are too busy with work <u>to help out</u>. (noun; adverb)
15. I have so many notes <u>to review</u> and old tests <u>to study</u>! (adjective; adjective)
16. I want <u>to go to the zoo</u>, because I love <u>to see all the different animals</u>. (noun; noun)
17. The dog was barking loudly, so her owners rushed outside <u>to check on her</u>. (adverb)
18. Fantasy authors write <u>to interest their readers</u> and <u>create a magical world</u>. (adverb; adverb)

Diagramming Exercises:

1. To be a famous actor is his only goal.

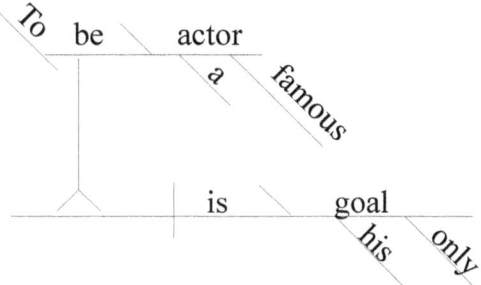

    The infinitive phrase *to be a famous actor* is the subject of the sentence. *To be* is the infinitive. *Goal* is a predicate nominative of the linking verb *is*.

2. I like to jog in this neighborhood before sunset.

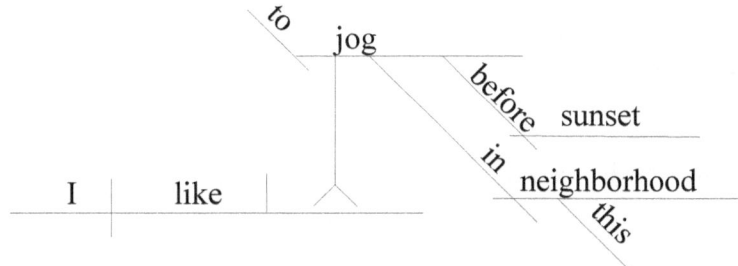

    The infinitive phrase *to jog in this neighborhood before sunset* is the direct object of the verb *like*. (<u>What</u> do I like? *To jog*.)

3. Wilma decided to give her favorite vintage necklace to her loving granddaughter as a gift.

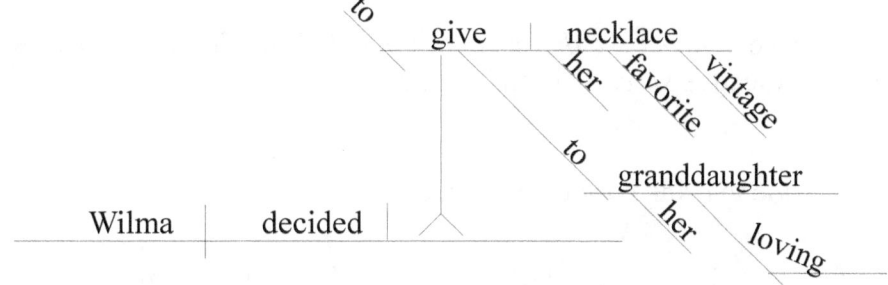

    The infinitive phrase *to give her favorite vintage necklace to her loving granddaughter* is the direct object of the verb *decided*. *Loving* is a present active participle. (<u>What</u> did Wilma decide? *To give etc.*)

4. The purpose of this silly example is to teach diagramming infinitives.

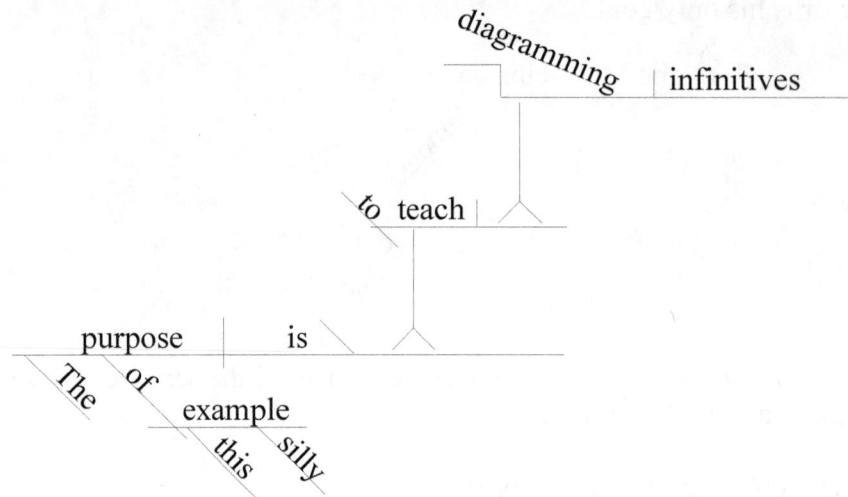

The infinitive phrase *to teach diagramming infinitives* is a predicate nominative. *Diagramming* is a gerund taking the direct object *infinitives*.

5. Be sure to lower the thermostat in the kitchen after dinner.

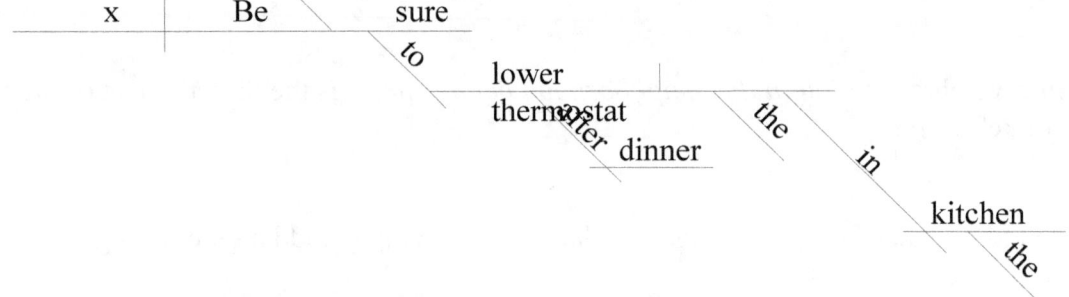

The infinitive phrase *to lower the thermostat in the kitchen after dinner* serves as an adverb modifying the predicate adjective *sure*. *Be* is an imperative.

6. It is much too hot outside to drink coffee, tea, and cocoa.

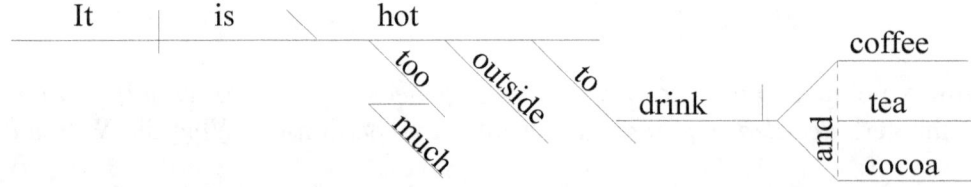

The adverbial infinitive phrase *to drink coffee, tea, and cocoa*, modifies the adjective *hot*. The adverbs *too* and *outside* also modify *hot*, and the adverb *much* modifies *too*.

7. Many of my friends with licenses like to and are allowed to drive their cars to school each day.

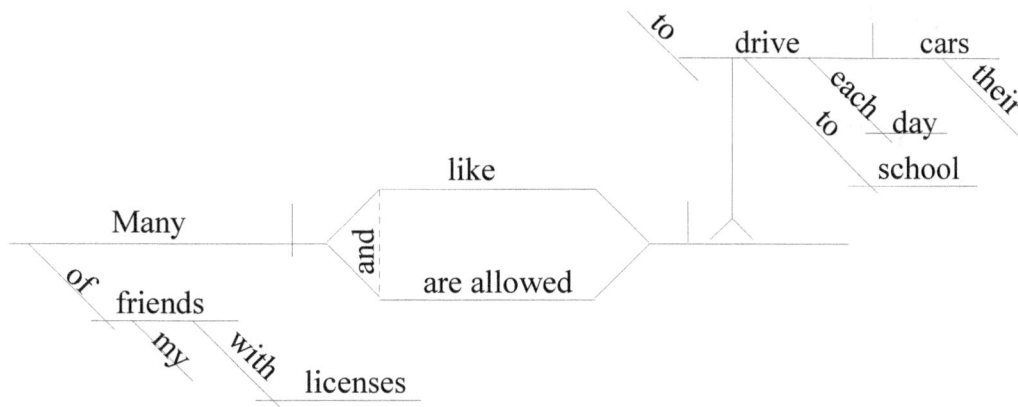

The infinitive phrase *to drive their cars to school each day* is the direct object of both *like* and *are allowed*. *Each day* is an adverbial objective.

8. Our teachers do not let us, their students, put our aching feet on our desks during class.

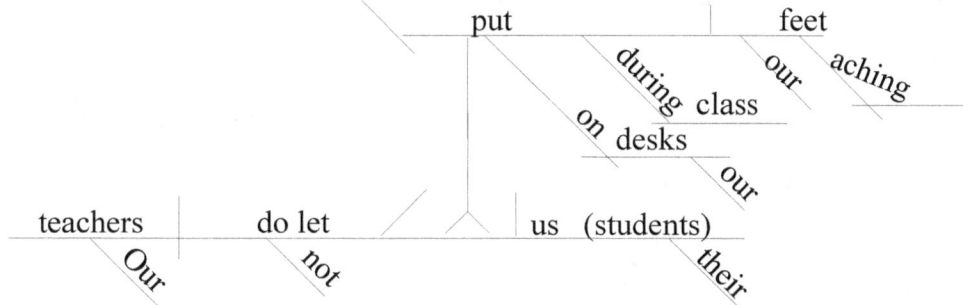

The infinitive phrase *put our aching feet on our desks during class* serves as an object complement. When an infinitive is used as an object complement following *let*, there is no *to* before the infinitive. *Aching* is a participle. *Students* is in apposition with *us*, the direct object.

9. Studying physics makes me want to ram my head against a wall repeatedly.

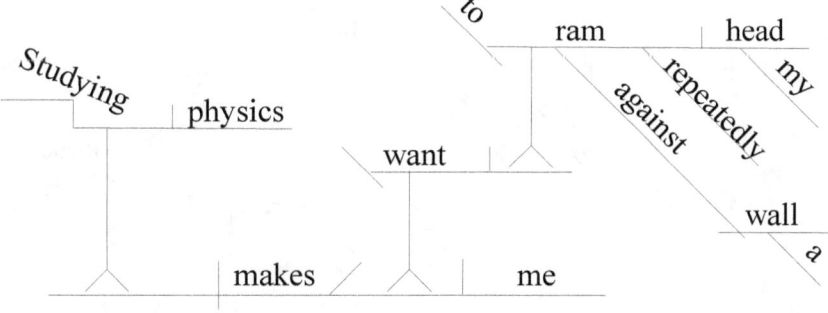

In this sentence, an infinitive phrase is being used as an object complement after the verb *make*. When this happens, the infinitive (*want*) is not preceded by *to*. The other infinitive phrase, *to ram my head against a wall repeatedly*, is the direct object of *want*, the first infinitive. *Studying physics* is a gerund phrase and is the subject of the sentence.

10. I am unable to assist you further.

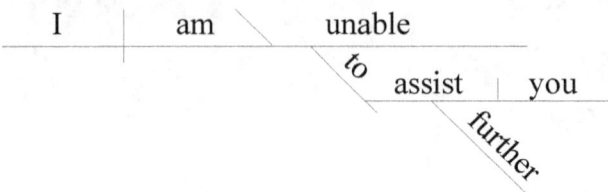

The adverbial infinitive phrase *to assist you further* modifies the adjective *unable*. *Further* is an adverb.

11. Patricia, despite her hostile and aggressive manner, wants nothing but to have friends.

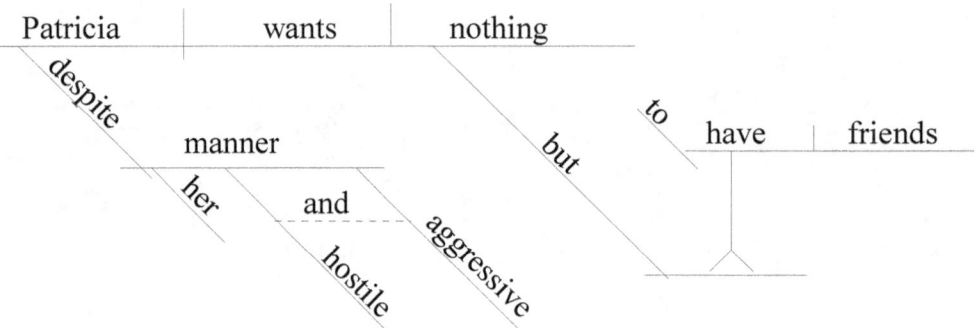

This sentence's infinitive phrase, *to have friends*, is the object of the preposition *but*. *Despite* is a preposition.

12. I have several interesting books for her to read over the course of the year. *Her* is the subject of the infinitive *to read*. The entire infinitive phrase is the object of the preposition *for*.

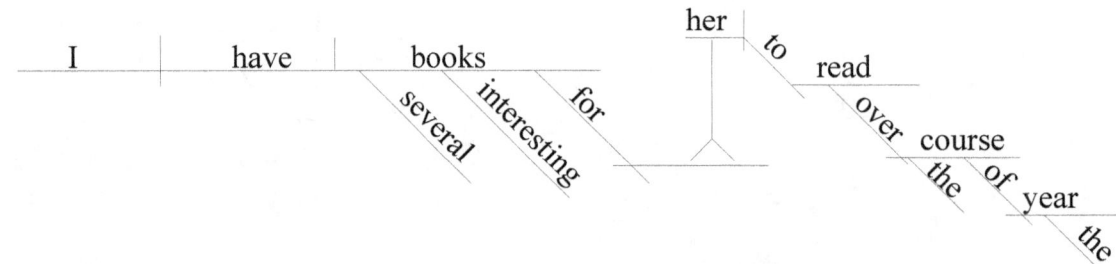

The object of the preposition *for* is not only *her*, but rather *her to read over the course of the*

year. Her, in the objective case following the preposition, is the subject of the infinitive *to read*.

13. It was truly unnecessary for you to call me those rude names with my boyfriend standing there.

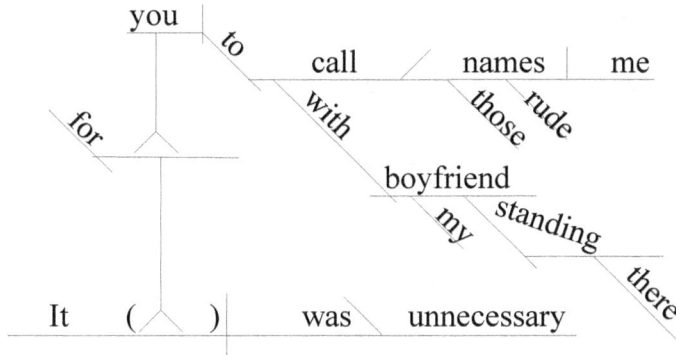

The phrase *for you to call me those rude names with my boyfriend standing there* is in apposition with the sentence's subject, *it*. We diagram *for* as though it is introducing a prepositional phrase. *You* is the subject of the infinitive *to call*. *Names* is an object complement. *Standing* is a present active participle. *There* is an adverb.

Chapter 9: Clauses

Exercise 1:

1. <u>When you finish reading the book</u>, <u>you should try reading this one</u>.
2. <u>I don't know</u> <u>how warm it is outside</u>.
3. <u>The man</u> <u>who wrote the book</u> <u>died before it was published</u>.
4. <u>Please put away your dishes</u> <u>after you wash them</u>.
5. <u>Walking to the store, the young boy tripped</u> <u>when he stubbed his toe</u>.

Exercise 2:

1. that 2. which 3. whom 4. which 5. that 6. where 7. that 8. which 9. whose 10. who 11. whom 12. which

Exercise 3:

1. You'll never guess <u>what I did today</u>. (direct object)
2. <u>What I did</u> bothered my family. (subject)
3. <u>That he didn't know how to cook</u> was quite obvious. (subject)
4. I love tasting <u>whatever other people think is good</u>. (direct object)
5. From <u>what you are telling me</u>, I cannot make an accurate diagnosis. (object of preposition)
6. I know <u>that purple is the color of royalty</u>. (direct object)
7. He told me <u>what he knew</u>. (direct object)
8. Martha knew <u>what he said was true</u>. (direct object)
9. His problem is <u>that he is a procrastinator</u>. (predicate nominative)
10. Joy loves <u>that her dog is small</u>. (direct object)
11. Allie reads <u>whatever books she can find</u>. (direct object)
12. Some people say <u>that aliens exist on Mars</u>. (direct object)
13. Your issue was <u>that you were not assertive enough with your boss</u>. (predicate nominative)
14. <u>What you are looking at right now</u> is a very famous painting. (subject)
15. A good secretary sees <u>what needs to be done</u> and does it. (direct object)
16. I don't know <u>whether it will snow tomorrow.</u> (direct object)

Exercise 4:

1. You will find the answer <u>that you are looking for in this book</u>. (ADJ)
2. <u>Until the criminal spends twenty years in jail</u>, he will not be allowed to leave. (ADV)
3. The pond <u>where the frogs live</u> is also inhabited by grasshoppers. (ADJ)
4. Show me <u>that you are not a coward</u>. (N)
5. I would like to eat <u>whatever you would like to serve me</u>. (N)
6. <u>While I was walking to the store</u>, I bumped into my neighbor. (ADV)
7. What is it <u>that you need</u>? (ADJ)
8. The boy turned on the stove, <u>even though his mother warned him not to</u>. (ADV)
9. Number 5 is the problem <u>that you answered incorrectly</u>. (ADJ)
10. Carlos always appreciates <u>what his family gives him</u>. (N)
11. <u>Provided that you eat healthily and work out</u>, you will stay in good shape. (ADV)
12. Reading novels, <u>which is a good way to expand your vocabulary</u>, can be fun as well. (ADJ)

13. That she was unprepared was evident. (N)
14. My grandmother believes that no one ever actually landed on the moon. (N)
15. I left my house after the rain subsided. (ADV)
16. I don't know the man about whom you are talking. (ADJ)
17. Believe in what you think is right. (N)
18. Is your sister the person whom Jeremy is taking to the dance? (ADJ)
19. As soon as Mike finishes playing his game, we will go out to dinner. (ADV)
20. The police officer claimed that the driver of the red car was at fault. (N)
21. Sometimes James's father acts as if he is a dictator. (ADV)
22. Sara told me the address to which I should send the letter. (ADJ)
23. I know that Jim hates spaghetti. (N)
24. Unless Dan first admits he has a problem, he will not be able to fix it. (ADV)
25. I need to find the girl whose wallet I have. (ADJ)
26. Greg found what you were looking for. (N)
27. Answer the phone that is ringing! (ADJ)
28. Before you leave for lunch, make sure you have some money. (ADV)
29. Ryan told Susan where the cookies from the jar went. (N)
30. The baby cries whenever she needs something. (ADV)

Diagramming Exercises:

1. Fran failed the test because she had not studied.

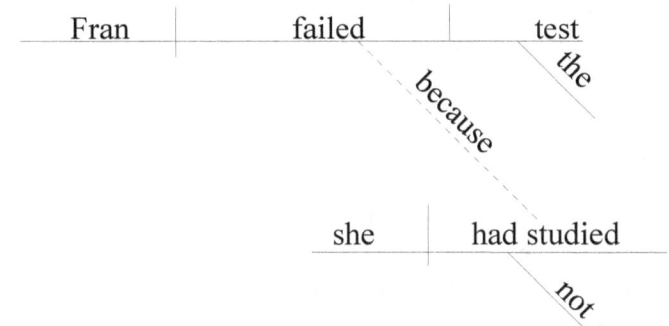

This sentence contains two clauses: the independent clause *Fran failed the test* and the subordinate adverb clause *because she had not studied*, introduced by the subordinating conjunction *because*. We connect the two clauses at their verbs (*Why* did she fail? *Because she had not studied.*)

2. Although they elected him president, they did not consider him a good man.

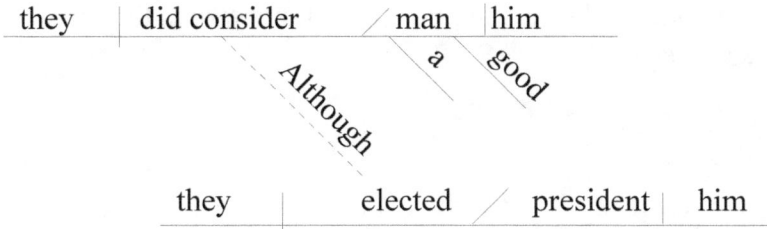

The adverb clause *although they elected him president* is introduced by the subordinating conjunction *although*. Both clauses contain objective complements. [*not* belongs on a slanted line below "did consider] ???

3. Unless jogging makes you too tired, you should try it someday for exercise.

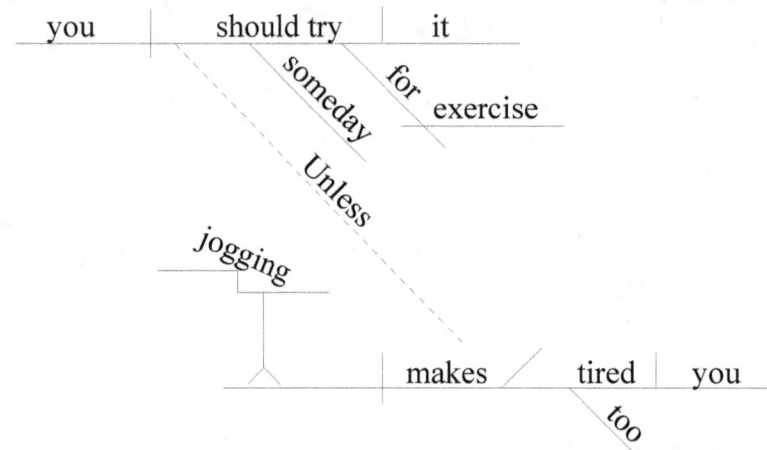

The adverb clause *unless jogging makes you too tired* is introduced by the subordinating conjunction *unless*. *Jogging*, the subject of the subordinate clause, is a gerund.

4. If I give you some money, will you run to the store for a few groceries that I need?

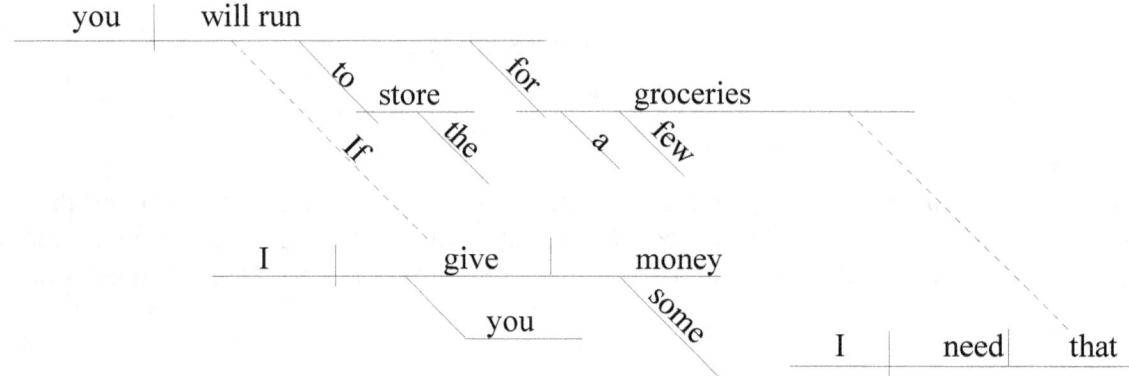

The adverb clause *if I give you some money* is introduced by the subordinating conjunction *if*. This sentence also contains a relative clause; the relative pronoun *that* is the direct object of the relative clause and its antecedent is *groceries*.

5. Your sister will come to your recital, even if she must miss her favorite show on TV.

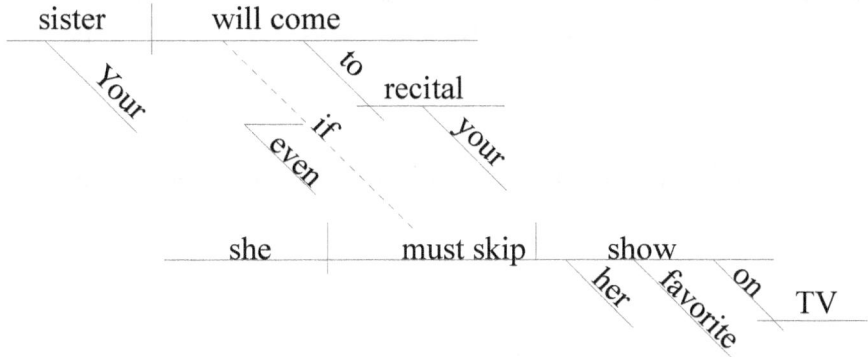

The adverb clause *even if she must skip her favorite show on TV* is introduced by the subordinating conjunction *if*, which is then modified by the adverb *even*.

6. Because my brother's current roommate seems friendly and converses well, we invited him to dinner.

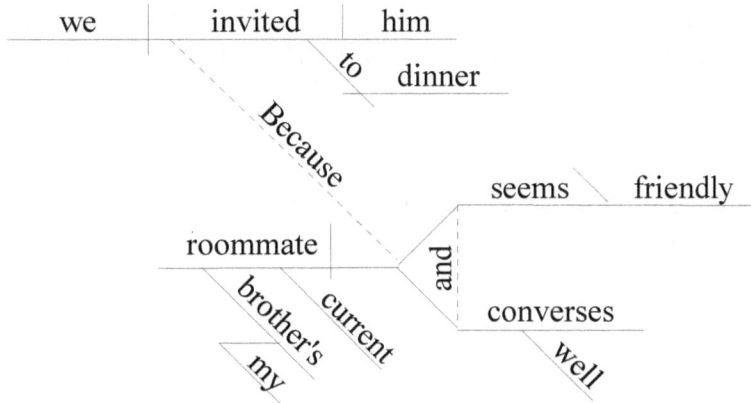

The adverb clause *because my brother's current roommate seems friendly and converses well* is introduced by the subordinating conjunction *because*. The possessive noun *brother's* is diagrammed as an adjective; *my* further modifies it.

7. The dancing bear that you saw in the zoo just had a baby!

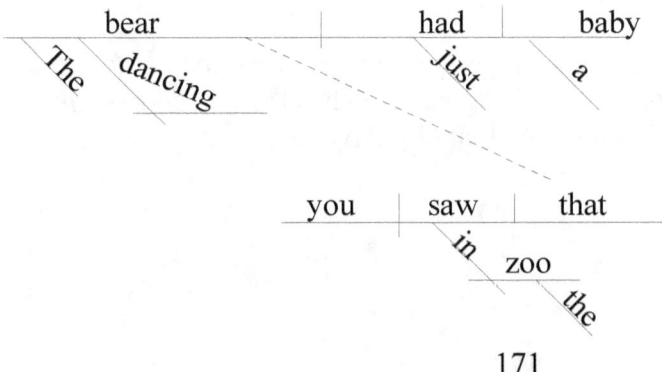

171

This sentence contains the relative (adjective) clause *that you saw in the zoo*. The relative pronoun *that* is the direct object of this relative clause. Its antecedent is *bear* (the subject of the main clause). *Dancing* is a participle. *Just* is an adverb.

8. Evan gave Priscilla, who was his first girlfriend, a beautiful bouquet of blooming roses.

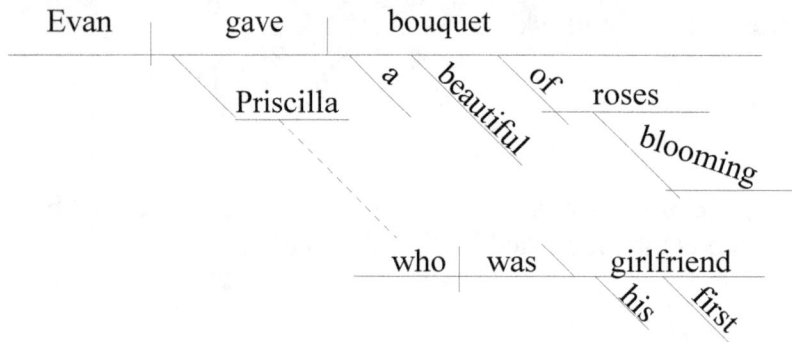

This sentence contains the adjective clause *who was his first girlfriend*. The relative pronoun *who* is the subject of the relative clause. Its antecedent is *Priscilla* (the indirect object of the main clause). *Blooming* is a participle.

9. Is that the girl whose parents you met last week at graduation?

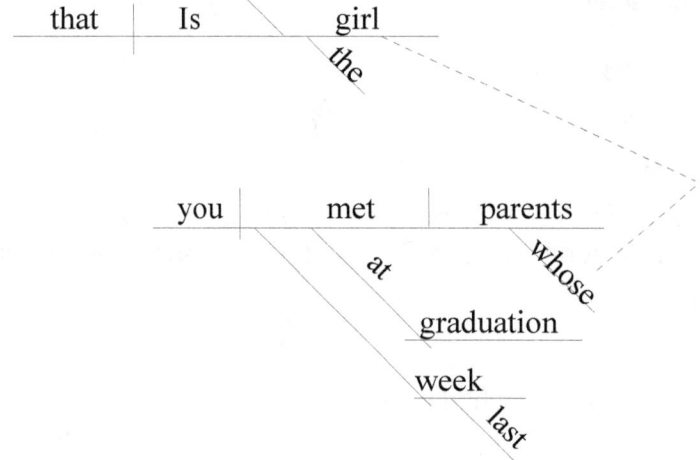

This sentence contains the adjective clause *whose parents you met last week at graduation*. The relative pronoun *whose* (the possessive form, modifying *parents*) has the antecedent *girl* (the predicate nominative in the main clause). *Last week* is an adverbial objective.

10. Can you direct this message to the mailbox of the person to whom it is addressed?

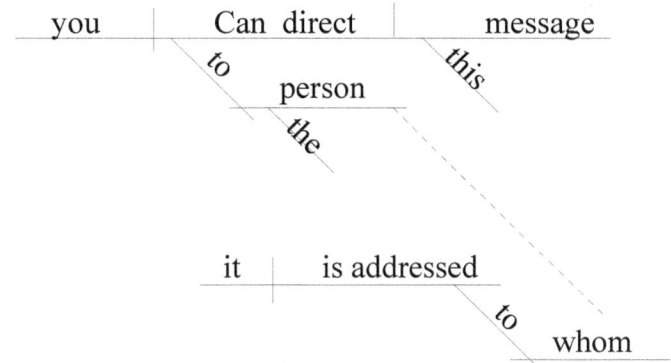

This sentence contains the adjective clause *to whom it is addressed*. The relative pronoun *whom* is the object of a preposition in the relative clause. Its antecedent is *person* (the object of a preposition in the main clause).

11. That's the thing I was going to tell you about.

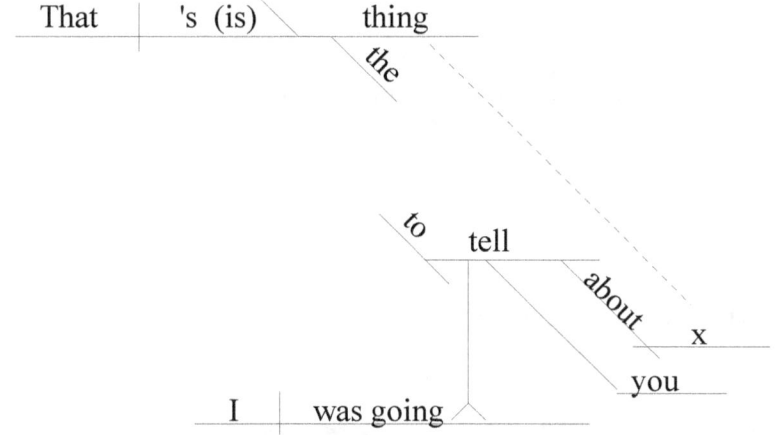

This sentence contains the adjective clause *I was going to tell you about*. This adjective clause, however, is different than others that we've seen because the relative pronoun *which* has been omitted. We call this the *unexpressed relative pronoun*. In this case, the unexpressed relative pronoun *which* would have been the object of the preposition *about*, and so we place an *x* where it would have been. Its antecedent would have been *thing* (the predicate nominative in the main clause). Had we included *which*, the sentence would have read: *That's the thing about which I was going to tell you*, which is grammatically correct, but overly formal for everyday conversation.

12. I won the race because I was the one who swam fastest.

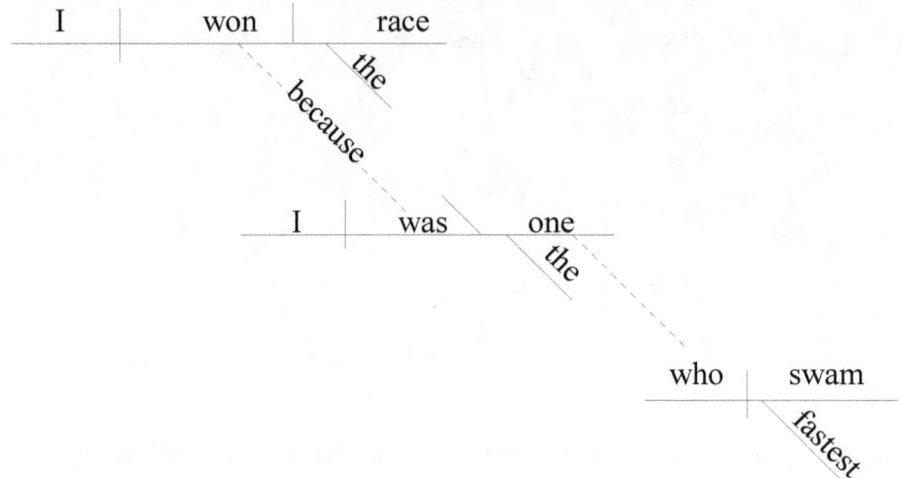

This sentence contains both an adverb clause and an adjective clause. The adverb clause *because I was the one* is introduced by the subordinating conjunction *because*. The relative clause *who swam fastest* contains the relative pronoun *who* as the subject. The antecedent of *who* is *one* (the predicate nominative of the adverb clause).

13. I know that you are a diligent and hardworking student.

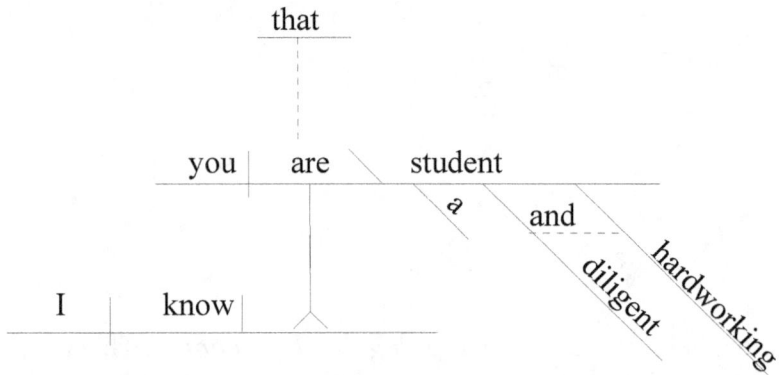

The noun clause *that you are a diligent and hardworking student* is the direct object of the verb *know*. *That* serves the purpose of introducing the noun clause, but it has no real meaning; it could just as easily be omitted.

14. My biggest problem is that I do not have time for skiing or swimming, my favorite activities.

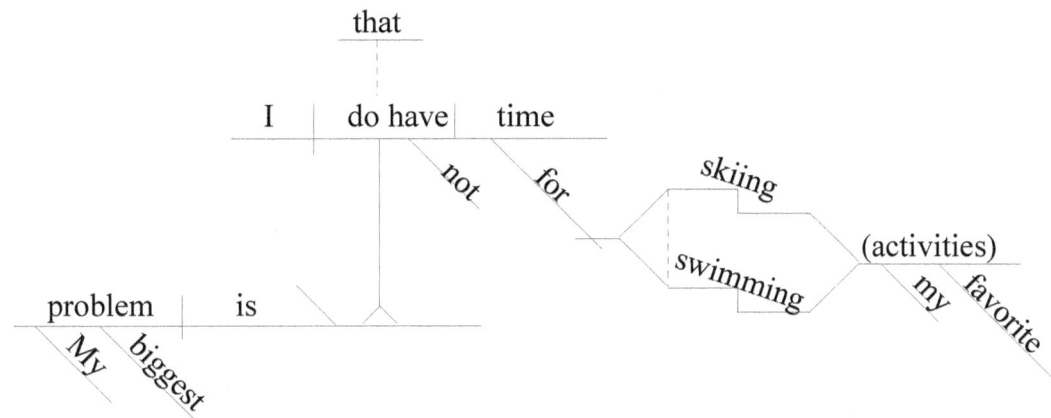

The noun clause *that I do not have time for skiing and swimming, my favorite activities* is a predicate nominative. *Skiing* and *swimming* are gerunds, and *my favorite activities* is in apposition with them both. *That* introduces the noun clause. ??? [need *and* on the dotted line connecting *swimming* and *skiing*]

15. It is unlikely that many people will come to the performance late.

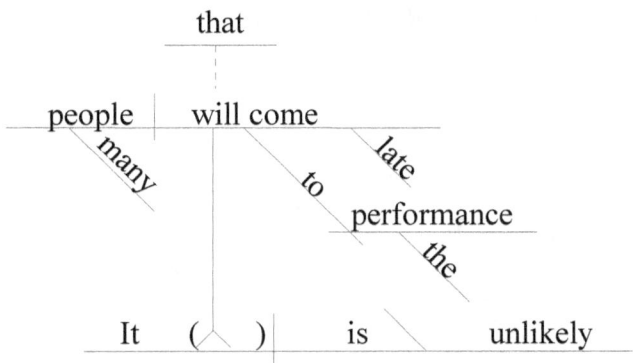

The noun clause *that many people will come to the performance late* is in apposition with the sentence's subject, *it*.

16. Yesterday we asked them whether we should give a dollar to the laughing musician who played guitar nearby.

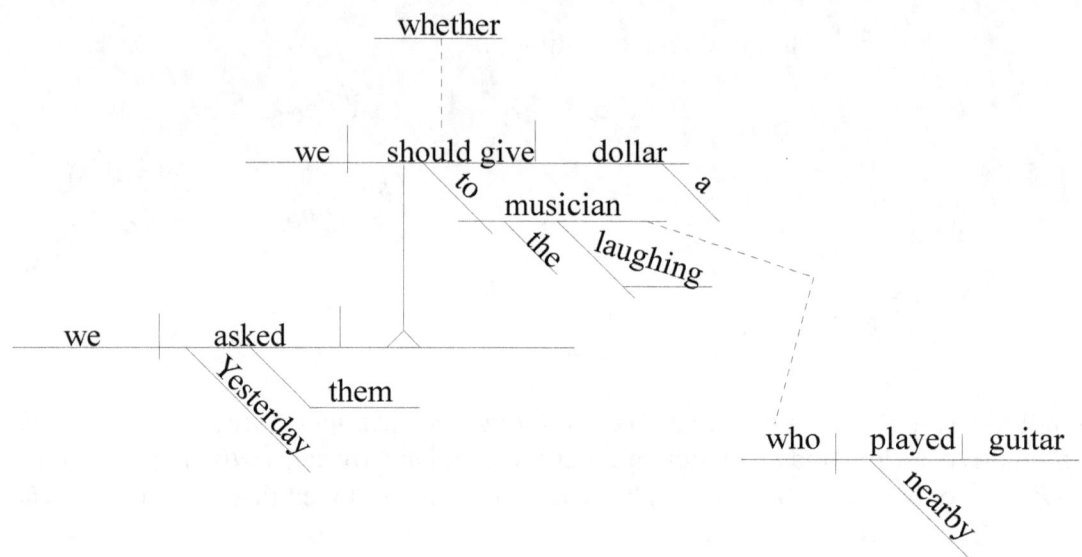

This sentence contains both a noun clause and an adjective clause. *Whether* introduces the noun clause *whether we should give a dollar to the laughing musician*, which is an indirect question that acts as the direct object of the verb *asked*. The relative pronoun *who* serves as the subject of the relative clause *who played nearby*. The antecedent of *who* is *musician*.